As you set out on the way to Ithaca
hope that the road is a long one,
filled with adventures, filled with discoveries.
—C. P. Cavafy, 1910

ANN GETTY
INTERIOR STYLE

BY DIANE DORRANS SAEKS

Photography by Lisa Romerein

ANN GETTY
INTERIOR STYLE

BY DIANE DORRANS SAEKS

RIZZOLI
NEW YORK

New York · Paris · London · Milan

CONTENTS

A SERIOUS COLLECTOR OF RARE AND HISTORIC textiles, Ann Getty scooped up the best of eighteenth-century Prelle silk brocades (similar to those hand woven for Versailles and the Louvre) and found fragments of English silks, some of them originally handcrafted for ball gowns and dresses. These fragments were pieced together for the pillows on the living room sofa, *previous pages*. The larger pillows display "bizarre" patterns inspired by Chinese motifs. Paintings include a Gustav Moreau at left, a charming Renoir, and an Impressionist snow scene by Pissarro.

IN HOMAGE TO CRAFTSMANSHIP and connoisseurship, Ann and Gordon Getty created a lifetime's collection of museum-worthy furniture and paintings displayed in their living room, *opposite*. Tables and chairs gleam with gilded carving and silken antique textiles, and a new overmantel by Agrell Architectural Carving demonstrates the uplifting power of beauty. Included are: a pair of early-eighteenth-century giltwood armchairs designed by John Vardy for Spencer House, London; early George III carved giltwood armchairs; and a George II giltwood chair from the collection of David Garrick. The chair seats and backs are upholstered with of-the-period silk brocades. The (functioning) French Imperial silver-gilt library table lamp, center, by Martin-Guillaume Biennais, Paris, 1809–19, is adorned with the applied arms of Napoleon's mother. A similar one is in the collection of the Louvre.

INTRODUCTION
by Diane Dorrans Saeks

Ann and Gordon Getty's stately Willis Polk–designed residence is almost invisible behind a fragrant blur of blooming magnolia trees and jasmine vines. It stands very discreetly on an ultra-private hillside in San Francisco, with views of the Golden Gate Bridge, the Palace of Fine Arts, and silvery expanses of San Francisco Bay.

At a distance, the tranquil scene is framed by the deep-green forest of the Presidio, and as the late-afternoon fog whirls, scents of cedar and eucalyptus trees blend with the tang of sea air into a distinctive and bracing atmosphere.

It's a life away from the spotlight. But museum curators, art collectors, antiques connoisseurs, and cognoscenti in many fields arrive here for just one reason: the Gettys' extraordinary and world-class art and antiques collection, and the splendor of their interiors.

Rooms are infused with the brilliance of a lifetime's collection that includes large-scale canvases by Canaletto and Bellotto; intimate scenes by Cassatt, Vuillard, and Matisse; and Odilon Redon's vivid and uplifting floral portraits.

Northern light refracts shards and shimmers from jeweled Russian chandeliers, rock-crystal lamps, mirrored cabinets, the intricate gilt-bronze of Boulle chests, acres of *verre églomisé*, fine examples of French and English craftsmanship, and Ann Getty's design bravura.

Beside a pedimented cabinet hangs a Degas portrait of a woman in a feather-trimmed hat. A small, deft Matisse canvas captures the moment when the sun diffuses tender early-morning light in an olive grove on a hillside above Nice.

The collection is personal, the result of focused decades of research, study, consultation with experts, sleuthing, and exacting standards. Ann Getty's taste for quality, charm, beauty, and the rare and eccentric is evident in every room of the residence.

The interiors are spacious and the ceilings tall, but Ann Getty's meticulous attention to detail and the many delights of her clustered collections give the rooms an intimate feeling. It's this personal view, the reflection of private interests, and years of pursuit that fascinate the experts. Guests are entranced observers and participants in the tableau.

Vectors of brilliance energize each piece in the Getty residence—as well as the interiors that Ann Getty designs for clients.

Almost concealed behind a vivid tableau of porcelain court ladies flirting with boys in emerald jackets is a small marquetry box, circa 1748, by the great Italian cabinetmaker Pietro Piffetti. It's a rococo tour de force of carved ivory, tortoiseshell, mother-of-pearl, tulipwood, and ormolu.

"I was in New York to preview the portrait of Nijinsky by Jacques-Emile Blanche at Christie's," said Ann Getty. The portrait was in the private viewing room along with this little coffer.

"I was focused on the painting, but when I spotted the Piffetti piece I fell in love with it," she added. "He was the Ebanista Reale to the King of Sardinia, and most of his pieces are on a larger scale. I am happy to have this little treasure that displays the beautiful fluidity and technical skill for which he is known. It is a little gem that can sometimes go unnoticed."

And while curators admire the quality, precision, and rarity of the Getty collection, Ann and Gordon Getty find living with these personal favorites to be an everyday pleasure.

"I cherish most of the pieces in our collection and I am always thrilled when I can reunite items that originally belonged together. I love pairs of objects. I like paintings with associations, like the painting of Nijinsky (which I acquired after the viewing) by Jacques-Emile Blanche in the living room that relates to Rudolf Nureyev's collections in the music room," said Getty. "If I had to pick my favorite piece of furniture it would be the reverse-painted-glass cabinet that is in the dining room in my Sacramento Valley country house [pages 142–3]. It is English and dated around 1760. It is not the most important piece in the collection, but I think it is one of the most beautiful. Delicately depicted Chinese court scenes on reverse-painted glass cover the upper section of the breakfront. These mirror paintings are exquisite and magical in candlelight."

Many favorite pieces of art are in the master bedroom of the Pacific Heights residence. "I am very fond of Mary Cassatt's *At the Theater*," said Getty, whose collection includes several small paintings of mothers and children. "I admire the way Cassatt captured a young woman seated in a private box, her sense of anticipation, as well as the gentle depiction of the subject. She looks like she is caught up in the performance, but you can't read her exact expression. It is so complex and attentive; you don't know what she is thinking. It was originally owned by Paul Gauguin, and I am happy to have it now. I hang it in my bedroom so that I can look at it every day."

Ann Getty quietly caught the attention of leading art collectors, auction houses, and curators when she first started acquiring spectacular pieces from English country house sales in the 1970s.

San Francisco's elegant grande dame Denise Hale has known Ann Getty since Billy Getty was three years old. She is now the godmother of Billy and Vanessa's son, Alexander.

"In San Francisco society, Adolphus Andrews was the last of the social Old Guard with a significant collection of fine art and antiques—and subsequently I was so impressed by Ann's knowledge. She found the best advisors, and acquired the best of the best," said Hale. "She has had my deepest admiration from day one."

Similarly, Getty's serious approach, her studious tendencies, and her goal to create a personal and cohesive collection brought her to the attention of leading auction houses, a reciprocity that continues today.

"What most distinguishes Ann Getty's collecting passion is her connoisseurship in several, often very esoteric, fields of interest," said Warren P. Weitman, Jr., chairman of Sotheby's North and South America. "She achieves a harmony among art and antiques and history as she blends them together with her antique textiles, furniture with historical importance, and paintings by French Impressionist artists."

With her depth of knowledge and distinctive taste, Ann Getty has created the ambience of a magnificent English country house in an urban, sophisticated California environment, noted Weitman.

"The house in San Francisco transcends the city and travels to European culture at its pinnacle with well-chosen carpets, high-style English furniture with impeccable and historic provenance, important Old Master and French paintings," added Weitman. "Grand rooms are transformed into exquisite and authentic vignettes. Her devotion to detail and her care and discrimination make Mrs. Getty's command of interiors comprehensive and vital."

Ann Getty, distinguished by her elegant reticence, spends her time working on interiors for clients (including new clients in China). At her art studio, she studies and tests arcane techniques and materials and oversees antique textile restorations, and in the evening she is most likely poring over rare volumes or recherché auction catalogs.

In spite of common perception, she is far from a socialite.

"I used to go out once a month just to maintain this 'status,'" she joked. Now, it's all work, with high-level supervision of her Ann Getty Home collection, collaborations with decorative artists, and travel to studios and secret sources.

One delight of her firm has been working with bright, young couples in San Francisco and beyond. Getty's roster of clients—San Francisco families, high-tech couples, and entrepreneurs with houses in California, New York, and Hawaii—has always been ultra-private, but now Getty is in high demand. She recently completed the remodel and redesign of a house for son Peter, a musician, and has consulted on residential developments in Asia.

For herself and her clients, Getty is especially adept at creating mood as well as a cohesive story for each room. She loves chinoiserie, French craftsmanship, and Venice. The English chairs, Canalettos, and Bellottos in her music room look for all the world like the collection of an eighteenth-century lord who has returned from a Grand Tour in France and Italy.

After Getty launched Ann Getty & Associates in 1995 she followed with her Ann Getty House collection of forty-five ornately carved chairs, versatile tables, decorative objects, overscale upholstered ottomans, and copies of her favored desks. The standouts for connoisseurs of the collection are the reproductions of her 'Badminton' chairs, with their quirky Orientalist angles.

"I'm totally hands-on," says Getty. "I've been very practical and take-charge since I was a girl growing up on a farm in the Sierra foothills, picking peaches, helping in the walnut orchards, driving tractors, fixing things."

Before she launched her firm, Ann Getty spent decades devoted to international art and antiques studies at UC Berkeley, taking trips into remote corners of Ethiopia on paleoanthropology digs, and to hidden corners of China, India, and Egypt to study and acquire antique ceramics and textiles. Her first major project was her residence in San Francisco.

"It is very rare to find a town house that has been furnished with so much taste, the result of discriminating acquisitions and thought," said Giles Waterfield, director of the Royal Collections Studies (under the auspices of Her Majesty Queen Elizabeth and the Prince of Wales) and former director of the Dulwich Picture Gallery. "While the house is never ostentatious, the quality of the works of art in many genres is consistently high."

Martin Chapman, curator of European Decorative Arts at the California Palace of the Legion of Honor museum in San Francisco, is a frequent visitor.

"The Getty collection is filled with marvelous objects that any museum would give their eye teeth to own," he noted. "It is the superb quality of the objects, but also Ann Getty's style. Everything is arranged in a concentrated manner that no museum would dare to do. In the drawing room, the delicate fretwork chairs from the Chinese bedroom at Badminton are set cheek by jowl with the majestic Lalive de Jully's shell cabinet, an icon of French neoclassicism, and alongside princely Boulle chests. This effect of compressed luxury is remarkable. Only the bravest and most knowledgeable collector would mix objects this way."

For Ernst-Ulrich Leben, associate curator of Waddesdon Manor, the Rothschild Collection, the French furniture assembled by Ann Getty presents examples of the best of French taste covering the period from Louis XIV to the reign of Louis XVI.

"It is not only the prestigious provenances, but the objects themselves are icons of the period's spirit at the moment of their creation," said Leben. "I especially admire the neoclassic ebony collector's cabinet, which simply is part of the set of prototypes that established the style 'goût grec', as early as 1756. Mrs. Getty has a preference for spectacular pieces with architectonic character such as the pair of console tables by Jacques Dubois, which in spite of their monumental design are delightfully refined pieces of furniture."

Today, the rooms of the Getty residence glow with baroque splendor and the accumulation of a life spent exploring design.

Over time, her taste has become more focused. In particular, recherché examples of chinoiserie and bold Coromandel screens enrich not only her residence but clients' interiors as well.

"I have used Coromandel screens in the living rooms of many residences, and fine examples of lacquer panels," said Getty.

"Coromandel screens give the rooms a rich, layered patterning. I've placed them behind sofas rather than artwork as they provide a beautiful and detailed backdrop. In my living room I incorporated fragments of a rare but broken screen into the architectural elements of the room."

"I am drawn to the great examples in any genre, whether furniture, textiles, rugs, or art, or something I don't even know about yet," she said. "I am not always actively looking, but when I see something exceptional in every way, it is irresistible—like the Pietro Piffetti coffer in my living room—and it may become part of the collection."

Getty is known for more traditional decor though she enjoys working with modern interiors for clients.

"We've incorporated modern elements and classic twentieth-century pieces into many of our recent designs, and I love the clean feeling of these spaces. In the future, embracing the technology of smart houses is inevitable, and I find the functionality of a truly modern interior to be intriguing."

Her scope of collecting continues to broaden.

"I will keep searching. I love the hunt and I especially love finding something exquisite, moving, rare, unexpected, and rich with history," added Getty.

Warren Weitman admires the panache of the designer's vision.

"Each room has the grace and comfort of historically important pieces, like the chairs from Spencer House, the chinoiserie chairs by John Linnell," he noted. "This remarkable journey through English and French and even Chinese history is done with the utmost taste and desire for comfort. Ann Getty has re-created and reinvented a world by preserving it and bringing it to life."

Chapter One

Gordon and Ann Getty Residence
San Francisco

A GROUP OF CIRCA-1750 LOUIS XV ORMOLU-MOUNTED CHINESE PORCELAIN FIGURES of court ladies, *previous pages*, supports candle nozzles and is flanked by birds with colorful plumage on rockwork bases. The ladies and the kneeling boys in yellow-enameled jackets are mounted on volute bases cast with foliate motifs, in the French taste. This collection, from the estate of Consuelo Vanderbilt Balsan, formerly the Duchess of Marlborough, stands on a table beside the large tufted sofa in the living room.

IN THE DINING ROOM, the alluring late-eighteenth-century Venetian mirrored cabinet stands on an ornate giltwood base, *opposite*. The cabinet, of exceptional quality and rarity, was formerly in the collection of Arturo Lopez Willshaw.

Perched on gilt sconces is a series of Qianlong (1735–95) Chinese porcelain figures, including elegant famille rose–style court ladies, all candleholders. A pair of circa-1775 Chinese porcelain figures of women holding trophies of good fortune, from the collection of Consuelo Vanderbilt Balsan, appears to be bestowing good luck to dinner guests. The geometric green, gold, and silver *verre églomisé* reverse-painted mirrored wall panels were created by Frances Binnington.

In the corner is a reflection of one of a pair of circa-1744 French gilt-bronze multi-branched girandoles (candelabra), perched on a Boulle *médaillier* (an eighteenth-century locked cabinet made for securing medals and precious jewels). The girandoles, originally commissioned for a grand salon overlooking the Place Vendôme, were formerly in the collection of the Antenor Patiño family and most recently in the collection of Hubert de Givenchy.

THE STORY OF ANN AND GORDON GETTY'S SAN FRANCISCO RESIDENCE and collections is a tale of style-conscious kings, ambitious emperors, power-hungry princes, connoisseur dukes, decorating duchesses, covetous counts, and the wildly extravagant Augustus the Strong of Saxony—all of them lifelong art patrons, decorators, and avid collectors of the decorative arts. In their mad dash to surround themselves with beauty, these historical characters commissioned furniture makers, artists, and all the great architects of their day. Their beautiful and museum-worthy objects—the marriage coffers, vivid paintings, porcelains, gilded mirrors, Sèvres vases, carved and gilded chairs, Boulle cabinets, and even miniature jade carvings they commissioned—now embellish the interiors of the Getty residence.

In every room of their house, including in their poetic guest rooms, the Gettys' collections offer arresting portraits and allegories of power and creativity. There are the treasures of such eighteenth-century rulers as George II, George III, Napoleon, a

Medici Pope, and a Chinese emperor or two, as well as the munificent landed gentry on their various acquisitive Grand Tours. From their estates and descendents, the Getty family has acquired pieces that reflect the workmanship, ingenuity and artifice of their era's most talented and expressive artists, creative cabinetmakers, weavers, carvers, goldsmiths, potters, glassblowers, and sculptors.

Through the family's extensive forty-year collection of Chinese export porcelains, Venetian paintings, French textiles, Sicilian painted glass chairs, Russian chandeliers, and Indian ivory desks are woven the far-flung threads of the history of world exploration; of early trade with China, Japan, and India; empires rising and falling; and the discovery of such rare materials as ebony and exotic woods, gems, and minerals.

In the living room on a graceful cabinet are a series of smiling, chic court ladies shaped in porcelain, holding candle nozzles, arrayed with merry boys in emerald jackets, made for the same emperor. Ann Getty loves to cluster pieces on a chest or tabletop.

THE ENTRY FOYER AND HALL are arranged for the delight of guests, but they also serve as a busy entrance and exit for designer Ann Getty coming and going with rolls of textiles, as well as restoration experts with their old-world art supplies, the family's active grandchildren, their beloved dogs, Yankee and Dandee, discreet security staff, friends, and museum curators. It's seldom quiet.

GUESTS ARRIVING FOR A DINNER PARTY walk along a pair of rare nineteenth-century Caucasian Karabaugh hand-knotted wood carpets, *previous page*. The circa-1740 giltwood and marble hall table features exuberantly carved scrolled panels and tendrils centered on an elephant mask. The chinoiserie figures are Meissen. The pair of circa-1745 giltwood chairs, with their original cut-silk velvet upholstery, was reputed to be part of the Buckingham House (later Buckingham Palace) collection. Cranes symbolize long life and appear in many guises throughout the house. Here, a collection of late-eighteenth-century Chinese export cranes (some holding fungi that symbolize good fortune) stand on George II carved giltwood brackets. The circa-1780 jeweled mechanical clock in the form of an ormolu oriental pavilion, by John Mottram, is a favorite of Denise Hale. The family has several other Mottram clocks.

GETTY FRIENDS RETURNING FROM A VISIT TO VENICE often stop and spend time looking at the superb eighteenth-century Canaletto painting *Entrance to the Grand Canal, Venice, Looking East*. It is a magisterial depiction of the basilica of Santa Maria della Salute, on the edge of the Grand Canal and anchoring the Dorsoduro *sestiere*. Canaletto captured the limpid Venetian light and the late-afternoon clouds hovering over the lagoon. Amazingly, this scene has hardly changed since the basilica, designed by architect Baldassare Longhena, was constructed in 1681. There are still gondolas moored at the bank, and now there's a busy vaporetto stop. The one significant change is that in 2009 the François Pinault Foundation opened a new contemporary art gallery in the fifteenth-century former salt warehouses, adjacent to the basilica. The brick wall, center, is now pierced by the entrance to the galleries, all remodeled with great elegance by Tadao Ando.

The provenance of this painting, like all art and antiques in the Getty collection, is noble, unique, and well documented. It first hung in Farnborough Hall, a 1684 Palladian-style limestone residence in Warwickshire, England. This and three other Canalettos of Venetian scenes were acquired in the mid-eighteenth century during a Grand Tour by William Holbech, grandson of the original owner of the stately home. The dining room on the south front of Farnborough Hall was redesigned to display these new paintings as well as works by the artist Giovanni Paolo Panini. The original paintings are long gone (this one has been in the Getty collection for several decades) and have been replaced by copies. The house and its landscaped gardens, now open to the public and managed by the National Trust, have experienced little alteration in the last two hundred years and remain largely as William Holbech left them.

HOVERING ABOVE THIS HALLWAY, *opposite*, is a Louis XVI ormolu, cut-glass, and enameled twelve-light chandelier. The enamel sphere is decorated with stars. The chandelier is reputed to have belonged to Josephine Bonaparte and hung in Malmaison. A pair of Chinese cloisonné cranes is from the nineteenth century. The William III green- and gold-japanned cabinet, circa 1695, is supported on a baroque giltwood stand with naked female caryatids on the foliate supports. The terra-cotta head, *above*, is Gandharan, fourth century AD.

THE LIVING ROOM SHIMMERS WITH HAND-WOVEN SILK, jade collections, woodcarving, antique textiles, and the glow of gold. As their tribute to beauty, connoisseurship, and fine craftsmanship, Ann and Gordon Getty brought together a lifetime's collection of museum-worthy furniture and paintings. The resulting multilayered room, in collaboration with LeavittWeaver, is sumptuous and seductive, carefully composed to offer moments of repose and delight. *Opposite*: The pair of *coffres de mariage* on stands is by Boulle. The pair of early-eighteenth-century giltwood armchairs, *above*, was designed by John Vardy for Spencer House, London. The portrait of Nijinsky in a Ballets Russes Siamese costume was painted circa 1910 by Jacques-Emile Blanche.

THE EXPRESSIVE *Paysage avec Cypres et Oliviers Environs de Nice*, 1918, by Henri Matisse, was originally in the Paris collection of Michael and Sarah Stein (Gertrude Stein's brother and sister-in-law). Matisse, in his early years in Nice, wrote of setting out to paint the countryside north of Nice at 5 a.m., to capture the subdued light on the olive and cypress trees. "The light is so delicate at this hour. It is like a paradise that one does not have the right to analyze." The circa-1740 green- and gold-japanned and carved giltwood cabinet, *opposite*, is attributed to Giles Grendey, one of the greatest eighteenth-century English cabinetmakers. It is crowned with a swan-neck molded pediment centered by a pierced, carved giltwood cartouche and a baroque cabochon. On the right of the cabinet is *Buste de Femme au Chapeau à Plume*s, 1887, by Edgar Degas.

Groupings are infused with charm: a scatter of jade sword handles, a stand of crystal obelisks, a carved miniature gondola beside an authentic Venetian antique lantern.

Getty has a vivid sense of wit and loves lighthearted decorative arts like bizarre Lyon silks depicting imaginary Chinese landscapes and temples. In the entry hall, two clusters of Meissen cherubic babies appear to be wearing hats made of cabbage leaves. All is not pomp and circumstance, after all.

The Gettys' Pacific Heights house was built shortly after the earthquake of 1906 to a classic design by architect Willis Polk.

Like many architects of the time, Polk incorporated a pastiche of English and French references (a bit of Adam, a dash of Soane, Louis-Louis) into a harmonious and timeless residence. Inspired by the great eighteenth-century English country houses, Getty, working closely with architect Ed McEachron, bestowed on the San Francisco house a bolder and more cohesive architectural distinction. Today, with the addition of an adjacent Palladian-style house that was integrated into the original, the residence gracefully offers a grand foyer and entry hall, an interior courtyard, and gracious, hospitable rooms where the Gettys, generous philan-

THE LARGE-SCALE, VELVET-UPHOLSTERED SOFA anchors the living room, its length and depth offering comfortable seating for as many as eight or more guests. Paintings include a Gustave Moreau, a petite Renoir portrait, and a Camille Pissarro snowy landscape. The empty space on the Chinese gauze–covered wall is usually filled by an 1888 painting of St. Martin-in-the-Fields by William Logsdail (shown on page 2), which was on loan for a museum exhibition. The pair of carved parcel giltwood and ebonized stools, upholstered with Bevilacqua silk velvet, is George II, circa 1740.

Ann and Gordon Getty have an expert curatorial staff headed by Deborah Hatch. Her responsibilities include research on paintings and antiques; hanging new works; supervising restoration and gilding; arranging loans to museum exhibitions; conducting tours for curators, directors, and museum groups; and maintaining a highly sophisticated security system.

thropists, entertain, as well as a series of private guest quarters.

At the time Ann Getty undertook her ambitious decade-long renovation, she mapped her own explorations, swooping on classical eighteenth-century English antiques; following the top international auctions; finding Sèvres vases, reverse-painted glass wall panels from a fantasy Chinese palace in Dresden, and Anglo-Indian inlaid ivory desks; and selecting dramatic gilded frames, chairs with character, and faded antique carpets. In the process, she developed a deep erudition of the inner workings of the auction world, antiques, and décor.

From auction sales of the great houses of England, Getty gathered George III giltwood mirrors attributed to John Linnell, as well as George II gilded chairs of a princely scale. "I love the fearless scale and guts of English antiques," said Getty. "They have personality. They bring so much character to a room."

Getty is especially adept at creating mood in her rooms. Just as eighteenth-century houses glowed with ormolu and delicate gilding, the San Francisco Bay house shimmers with baroque splendor.

There are elaborate gilded benches, museum-worthy chairs, a silk-upholstered glass Anglo-Indian chair with the look of carved crystal, Impressionist paintings, and delightful chinoiserie walls.

Now that the house is complete, and favorite Matisse paintings and rare porcelains have returned from museum shows, Ann Getty continues her design studies and her design projects. Beauty cannot wait.

ON A ROUND TABLE NEAR THE BAY-FACING WINDOWS in the living room is a "grand tour" of collections, including one of a pair of late-eighteenth-century Chinese celadon porcelain vases later mounted with a gadrooned ormolu rim, infant tritons, and laurel swags. The pair (the second is on the Gettys' winged cherub-ornamented table on page 39) was formerly in the collection of noted Ivorian leader Félix Houphouët-Boigny. The bowl and two Lucknow carved fish are rock crystal. *Opposite*: Ann Getty's favorite piece, a rococo ivory, mother-of-pearl, and tortoiseshell-inlaid coffer, circa 1748, by Italian Pietro Piffetti is partially visible at top left of the circa-1740 japanned and carved giltwood chest of drawers attributed to Giles Grendey. The surreal painting is by Gustave Moreau.

THE ENGLISH ROCOCO CARVED FIREPLACE SURROUND, in the manner of Chippendale, was commissioned by Ann Getty from Agrell Architectural Carving, Mill Valley, California, which specializes in custom woodcarving and architectural detail. It's a very eighteenth-century English concept, with Chippendale English baroque carving, magical and playful chinoiserie motifs, and fantasy court characters. Wood carver Adam Thorpe took 3,600 hours to complete the project in 1995. The intricate carving was undertaken in pine, with gesso applied by hand to give a softer and more malleable surface. The mantel and overmantel were recarved with finer detail before the piece was gilded, burnished, and then finished, incised, and distressed to look antique.

Also on view is a pair of porcelain sang de boeuf fu dog candelabra on carved gilt wall sconces, and, beside the fireplace, a pair of dark blue Sèvres vases on brass and ebony Boulle pedestals. The George II giltwood chair has its original velvet covering and was in the collection of Claus von Bulow.

ACANTHUS LEAVES, BIRDS, SCROLLS, RIBBONS, MOLDING, SHELLS, cartouches, and rococo flourishes were designed and carved by London-trained Adam Thorpe, considered the only carver up to the task of making this ambitious concept a reality. He first produced full-size drawings for Ann Getty to review, then he went to London to study how these chimneypieces were originally constructed (pretty crudely), and in particular how the different parts of the mirror would be constructed and attached (very cleverly). Study was also made of the strength and depth of the carving and its security and attachment to the wall. The green textile on the wall behind the carved sconce is antique Chinese gauze. Always respectful of intact antique textiles, Getty pieced together fragments of this gauze for the wall design.

THE JAPANESE ARITA PORCELAIN LEAPING CARP potpourri jars, circa 1700, were later mounted on Louis XV–style ormolu bases. The vase is Chinese celadon porcelain, late eighteenth century, with Louis XVI ormolu mounts. Among artists represented in the living room are Jacques-Emile Blanche, Camille Pissarro, Odilon Redon, Henri Matisse, Gustave Moreau, Auguste Renoir, Pierre Bonnard, and Giovanni Battista Tiepolo.

Fish, many versions and delights of chinoiserie, Asian motifs and decorative arts are recurring themes in Ann Getty's collections. Here, a pair of circa-1700 Arita Japanese porcelain figures of leaping fish balance on a rockwork and ormolu case as artful potpourri holders. The late-seventeenth-century carved and giltwood Sienna marble–topped English table is decorated with three winged cherubs, as well as swags of flowers, birds, and scrolled legs. The ormolu and celadon vase pairs with one on a nearby table. The jeweled clock is by Mottram. The wall panels are reproductions of fragments of Coromandel screens. Formerly in the collection at Elvaston Castle, Derby, England, the circa-1755 carved giltwood armchair is upholstered with patched antique fragments of "bizarre" silk brocade, hand woven in Lyon, France. Bizarre silks featured fantastical imagery inspired by the allure and exoticism of Asian ceramics and textiles and were used for costumes and decoration.

IN EVERY CORNER OF THE LIVING ROOM, Ann Getty has arranged pieces of great meaning and delight. Among her favorites are, top left, the late-eighteenth-century Chinese porcelain figures of kneeling boys. Above the velvet-tufted sofa, opposite, is a moody 1873 painting by Camille Pissarro, *Rue de la Citadelle, L'Hiver à Montfoucault, Effet de Neige*. The exquisite eighteenth-century carved Indian costumed figures on the table accompany a Chinese and Japanese jade collection. The pair of porcelain rabbits, so vivid they appear about to pounce, are early-eighteenth-century Japanese. A detail of a pair of circa-1740 carved parcel giltwood and ebonized stools shows Vitruvian scrolls, acanthus leaves, scallop shells, paw feet, and a fanciful ebonized elephant's head. They were formerly in the collection of Claus von Bulow. Ann Getty's connoisseurship and voracious studies have resulted in collections that are personal, unique, and ever evolving.

THE DINING ROOM IS LIKE A MAGICIAN'S CABINET FILLED WITH SURPRISES. One of the best-kept secrets is that the ultra-regal Louis XIV ormolu-mounted Boulle marquetry chest, dated 1700, is mounted on a concealed track and can move right or left at the touch of a hidden switch. It is attached to the large door panel behind it, which leads to the music room beyond. The door and chest are electronically programmed to slide silently to reveal or conceal the music room. The whole complex (and mysterious) system is hidden in a wall and did not in any way alter the integrity of the chest. (On pages 48 and 49, the sliding door is concealed in a wall panel and the space between the dining room and music room is open.)

The Kangxi porcelain jar depicts dragon boats similar to the miniature one adjacent to it on the chest top. The carved gilt mirror, 1765, is by John Linnell. The twelve-paneled mirrored chinoiserie walls, circa 1720, were originally designed for Augustus the Strong, King of Poland, Elector of Saxony, 1670–1733, for one of his Dresden palaces. The concept of decorative cabinets to display porcelain collections was very fashionable at the time. Ann Getty augmented the original to add shimmer and mystery with *verre églomisé* panels by Frances Binnington.

THE RESTAURATION ORMOLU, *tôle-peinte*, and glass eighteen-light chandelier once belonged to Hon. Mrs. Reginald Fellowes (Daisy). The glass lower section was crafted as a fish bowl, where the original owners kept live goldfish. The Getty family prefers a more decorative and humane concept: an 1890 Russian carved agate angel fish, with diamond eyes and a gold floating seaweed base. Guests in the know can gaze up and view it during dinner. The Regency inlaid veneered oak circular dining table, circa 1815, is attributed to George Bullock. The Louis XV giltwood chairs, circa 1740, are by Foliot (stamped N.Q. Foliot).

Court figures and settings with Canton famille rose dinner plates and settings, overleaf, are from the collection of Consuelo Vanderbilt, as well as Meissen pieces. Gordon Getty prefers clear glasses—so his wines are clearly visible—and occasionally more decorative crystal is used.

THE MUSIC ROOM, ADJACENT TO THE DINING ROOM, has a Russian theme that resonates with the English country house overview of the house. The hand-knotted wool rug is Russian, formerly in the collection of the Scottish Duke of Hamilton, who used it when he took over the Queen's Apartments at the Palace of Holy Roodhouse in Edinburgh in 1684. The patchwork curtains were from the estate sale of dancer Rudolf Nureyev's Paris apartment. The charmingly festive chandeliers include one original; the others are copies of an antique Russian lamp in the Getty collection. And the large-scale sofa, with its Bevilacqua custom-colored black and rose hand-woven velvet, is based on the double-sided sofas in Nureyev's Paris apartment. The nineteenth-century ottoman covered in a carpet of charcoal and olive green cut-silk velvet (one of a pair) was from the estate of the dancer. Rudolf Nureyev was a frequent visitor to the Getty residence and became a beloved friend of the family. The Russian National Orchestra, of which Gordon is a longtime patron, often plays in this room, to a full audience. Chairs for guests include copies of the Foliot original.

THE HISTORY OF EACH PIECE OF FURNITURE and art is of great interest to the Getty family. A painting or chair becomes compelling by virtue of its maker, its fine craftsmanship, and its provenance.

The mahogany and parcel-gilt chairs in the Music Room (adjacent to the window) are significant because they were designed by William Kent and belonged to George III's prime minister, Lord North, who lived at Wroxton Abbey. It was Lord North who first floated the idea for the Stamp Act and also the tea tax, so in effect the owner of these chairs was a catalyst for the American Revolution.

Paintings hanging here reiterate a Venetian theme that is apparent throughout the residence. Artists include Canaletto, Bernardo Bellotto (his nephew and pupil), and the Guardi family, who depicted scenes of Venetian life. The walls are covered with printed linen, which Getty painted and tinted to soften the color and give an antique patina.

AS HER CLIENTS NOTE, ANN GETTY HAS AN EXTRAORDINARY FILE OF RESOURCES, craftspeople, and talent of many kinds. These festive, five-foot-tall, Russian-style chandeliers are copies made in 1993 during the renovation/addition to the original house by Edgar McEachron. The designer was able to find glass blowers, crystal cutters, metal crafters, and the extraordinary workshop that orchestrated these lovely parts. With these festive lights illuminated, it feels like the party has begun. *Opposite:* The George III gilt-metal mounted Chinese lacquer cabinet, circa 1770, is attributed to Thomas Chippendale. The Chinese "plant" in a colorful jardinière on the stair is crafted in cloisonné and gilt bronze.

AT THE EAST END OF THE MUSIC ROOM is one of a pair of George II carved giltwood pier mirrors edged with foliate scrolls and clasps of flowers and leaves, originally made in 1755 for Hampden House, Buckinghamshire. A pair of late-eighteenth-century Russian neoclassical ormolu-mounted, white-marble, six-light candelabra is decorated with faceted pendants and ropes of cut-glass beads. The pair of George II carved giltwood and white-painted candlestands was crafted circa 1750. One of a pair of William IV striated Blue John (Derbyshire spar stone) urns stands on a George II carved giltwood pier table with a marble slab top. The design is attributed to Henry Flitcroft.

THE UPSTAIRS SITTING ROOMS, Gordon's studio and office, the bedrooms, and the guest quarters are utterly private, calm, and quiet. The downstairs rooms—the Music Room, dining room, and living room in particular—are used for musical soirees and entertaining. *Opposite:* An ormolu-mounted tulipwood and kingwood bow-fronted chest of drawers, circa 1765, is in the French taste. The floral oil paintings are two of the finest examples of work by French symbolist painter Odilon Redon (1840–1916). *Le Pavot Noir,* below, was originally sold by the Bernheim-Jeune Gallery in Paris. *Above:* The large and rare Chinese painted-wood Guanyin figure is tenth-twelfth century. The 1902 flower painting is by Henri Matisse.

THE HENRI MATISSE OIL PAINTING *Chrysanthèmes dans un vase de Chine* has been in the private collections of only three owners since it was first offered for sale at the Ambroise Vollard Gallery in Paris in 1904. Matisse at that time was considered an artistic outcast—collected by Gertrude Stein and her brother but derided by critics. Success followed many years later. This painting has been on public display just once, when Matisse's brushstrokes were barely dry. The circa-1680 Italian baroque cabinet, *opposite*, was crafted with an architectural silhouette and veneered in tortoiseshell framed in ivory. Figures and plaques in ivory ornament this bravura construction. It formerly belonged to Spain's Duke of Badajoz.

THE CIRCA-1770 PAINTED AND GILDED BED was designed by Thomas Chippendale for Edwin Lascelles at Harewood House, which remains the pre-eminent Chippendale country house. Chinoiserie remained immensely popular in stately English country houses, especially for bedrooms, and with the rise of neoclassicism the two styles were combined in quaint juxtaposition, as in this bed. The mahogany gueridon is German, circa 1800. Among the artists represented in the very personal collection in the bedroom are Balthus, Henri de Toulouse-Lautrec, Edgar Degas, and Mary Cassatt. The 1880 painting *Deux danseuses sur la Scene* on the neoclassical table, *above*, is by Edgar Degas.

THE ELABORATELY PAINTED ITALIAN LACCA POVERA and parcel-gilt bureau cabinet, circa 1740, was made for a Medici pope, whose crest is displayed. The top is fitted with figures depicting the four seasons. Paintings of landscapes, hunting scenes, birds, and animals on doors and drawer fronts continue the pastoral theme. A pair of arched, mirrored cabinet doors opens to reveal further doors, drawers, and pigeonholes. The Palais Royal ormolu and mother-of-pearl inkwell is French, circa 1820.

THE AMERICAN PAINTER MARY CASSATT (1844–1926) is one of Ann Getty's favorite artists. Many of her smaller and more intimate portraits hang in this bedroom. *Overleaf:* The pastel-and-gouache-on-paper *At the Theatre* was painted circa 1880 and first belonged to the artist Paul Gauguin. "Mary Cassatt has charm but she also has force," observed Gauguin. Edgar Degas was also a close friend and painted a notable portrait of Cassatt. Ann Getty loves associations in her art collection, and just below the Cassatt is a small Degas (see page 58). The circa-1720 German baroque white and blue lacquered cabinet balancing on a silver stand was formerly in the collection of John Paul Getty, London. The porcelain famille rose pieces are Chinese export, circa 1730–35.

ANN GETTY ACQUIRED THE EXQUISITE AND INTACT HAND-PAINTED, GILDED, and semiprecious stone–ornamented Syro-Turkish paneled rooms (circa eighteenth century) at auction in London. The jewel-encrusted wall panels were superbly carved and adorned with marble and colored stones. Getty and her team of architects, decorative artists, and specialists in historic and authentic restoration turned the many panels into a guest bedroom with an adjacent dressing room. Out of great respect for the integrity of the original, panels were added but the original pieces were left intact.

The design of the opulent mother-of-pearl and wood-inlaid bed is based on a throne at Topkapi palace in Istanbul. The headboard is decorated with ten very rare Qajar mirror paintings (*verre églomisé*) depicting delicate flowers, birds, and leaves. The Qajar dynasty ruled over the Persian Empire from 1796 to 1925.

The nineteenth-century sandalwood table, foreground, is Egyptian. A late-seventeenth-century Indian ivory and sheesham wood cabinet, right, balances on a George I cabriole-leg fruitwood stand. To add to the sultry mood, a painting by Eugene Delacroix of a Moorish tribal chief, paintings by Jean-Léon Gérôme, Henri Matisse drawings of his model in Moroccan costumes, Anglo-Indian eighteenth-century engraved ivory side chairs, and exquisite embroidered textiles are deployed throughout the suite. On the floor of the bedroom is a rare Bessarabian tapestry-woven carpet, circa 1890. The rooms are a treasure chest of exotica from India, Turkey, Egypt, and Persia.

In the paneled dressing room, the cut-glass crystal throne chair by F. &. C. Osler, with a crested back surmounted by three faceted bright-cut finials, was crafted in Birmingham, England, in 1894. The circa-1800 neoclassical green glass and mirror-inset dressing table, right, from the John Hobbs collection, was from the Villa Manin di Passariano de Codroipo (Udine), the largest and most extravagant villa in the Veneto.

THE CONSTANTINE GUEST SUITE is one of the new guest accommodations added to the Gettys' original residence when they acquired an adjacent house. The architectural renovation was directed by Edgar McEachron of McEachron Architects, who also supervised the renovation of Peter Getty's new residence.

In the bedroom, a George II carved and japanned mahogany tester bed offers a comfortable cocoon from which to view the bay and Alcatraz Island. All fabrics for the room were custom-designed with a Turkish theme. The pair of Indian ivory parcel-gilt chairs, circa 1790, is from Vizagapatam, a trade port on the Bay of Bengal where traditional South Indian motifs were incorporated into the manufacture of commissioned furniture in the English taste. Breakfast is served on a Flemish mother-of-pearl, pewter, ormolu, and tortoiseshell table, late eighteenth century. In the window, the pair of late-eighteenth-century ormolu and ivory desks is Russian, as is the ormolu-ornamented gueridon in the corner. London designer John Stefanidis advised on this room.

A PAIR OF CIRCA-1780 SICILIAN NEOCLAS-SICAL CHAIRS shimmer with gold-framed insets of etched *verre églomisé* painted to simulate precious gems and minerals, *previous pages*. Elegant and mysterious, the (somewhat fragile) chairs were made in the early eighteenth century for the very aristocratic Francesco Ferdinand Gravina, the fifth Prince of Palagonia, a fan of the ornate, for his Villa Palagonia. Located in the Sicilian coastal town of Bagheria, not far from Palermo, the Prince's baroque fantasy palazzo aroused the curiosity of travelers on the Grand Tour, including Sir John Soane and the German poet Goethe, during the eighteenth and nineteenth centuries. (The palazzo, privately owned, is still open to visitors and the rococo interior is intact.) Paintings in the bedroom and the Venetian-themed bathroom include costumes by Leon Bakst and *Petit Theatre* by James Ensor.

THE SUN-FILLED GUEST ROOM was named Josephine, an apt title for such a feminine and light-hearted suite. With its elegantly edited collection of Fantin-Latour flower paintings, a delightful painting of pink camellias by Paul Cezanne, and a series of portraits by Marie Laurencin, the room has a cohesive point of view and a tranquil air.

It is quite petite, so Ann Getty introduced a hint of grandeur with a George III–style painted tester bedstead with fluted columnar posts. The bed, from the estate of Sister Parish, is adorned with yards of lace, floral silk, and ruffles. The circa-1880 tapestry-woven carpet is Bessarabian.

A George I scarlet and gold japanned chinoiserie coffer-on-stand is decorated in gold and silver with dashing horsemen and attendants, temples, exotic birds, and nobles hunting a stag, all with foliate borders.

THE FRENCH ARTIST MARIE LAURENCIN (1885–1956) is one of Ann Getty's favorites, and this room and an adjacent hallway are animated by oil-on-canvas portraits of ballerinas and young girls holding bouquets, all painted in the early twentieth century. While some note the influence of painters like Pablo Picasso and Georges Braque and Cubists like Sonia Delaunay on her work, Laurencin created her own vocabulary of femininity with pastel colors and curvilinear forms.

PAUL CEZANNE'S 1880 PAINTING *Le Vase Bleu Sombre* was first exhibited at the famous Armory Show of 1913 in New York, *(above)*. The exquisitely composed tributes to roses by Henri Fantin-Latour *(opposite)*, who loved roses so much he even has a rose named after him, fill the bedroom with an ardor that is intensely romantic. Fantin-Latour (1836–1904) often painted single roses, and these opulent bouquets are rather rare. The George III carved mahogany writing table and cabinet, circa 1765, show the influence of Chippendale, with its open-work cornice and upright plinths supporting vase-form finials. Drawers have gilt-metal foliate escutcheons and pulls. The interior has a leather-lined writing surface.

THE JOSEPHINE GUEST BATHROOM CONTINUES ANN GETTY'S LOVE OF EMBELLISHMENT, with scrolls and flourishes of Victorian penwork and delicately rendered faux-ivory and ebony framing. The room, lacking architectural distinction, offers delight to the eye with a pair of brilliant *pietra dura* tables, along with *verre églomisé* panels of coral and seaweed. On the bath surround is one of three glass-domed shellwork floral bouquets, mid-nineteenth century, with elaborate flowers worked in seashells with wire supports. The Victorian-era octagonal hinged boxes are framed sailors' valentines, a West Indies tradition. The pair of French cartouche-shaped shellwork sconces is French.

THE POOL ROOM, WHICH OVERLOOKS A PRIVATE GARDEN, is a contemplative space for a quick dip and a moment of repose. But during Gordon's annual birthday party and other large celebrations, the pool is covered and becomes a dance floor. Bands of many styles—French cabaret, rock, garage, and vocalists—provide the fuel for corybantic moves. Then the pool room, vivid with multicolored lights and filled with sound, becomes a nightclub, a fantasy, and a pure escape. The doors are opened, and guests spill out to the garden, where a bar is set up. At midnight in Pacific Heights, there is no better place to be. The sinuous wrought-iron and steel French tufted chaise longue was crafted circa 1860.

A PAIR OF EAST INDIAN NACREOUS CEREMONIAL DOORS, early nineteenth century, is divided into geometric pierced fret panels backed by shimmering mica. On the door are eighteenth-century Balinese silver-gilt Kris (traditional ornamental dagger) handles. Highly important in Balinese society and spiritual life, these Kris handles in the form of a Raksasa are decorated with precious gems. The Raksasa in Hindu mythology is a grimacing demon or goblin that has the power to change shape at will and appear as animals, birds, or monsters.

Chapter Two

Residence of Peter Getty
Pacific Heights, San Francisco

runs along the entire west wing of Peter Getty's sun-filled residence. The interior was redesigned by Ann Getty in a bravura theatrical style, with newly painted faux-marble columns and cornices by decorative artist Shirley Robinson. A pair of 1940s French chandeliers, attributed to Jansen, is ornamented with beaded crystal drapery. The octagonal oak, marquetry, and parcel-gilt center table with three dolphin-form legs on a triangular plinth was originally in the seventeenth-century Ven House in Somerset (now a residence of Jasper Conran). The X-frame folding banqueting chairs, originally from the Palazzo Carraro Rizzoli in Milan, were reupholstered in elegant velvet by Sabina Fay Braxton, one of Ann Getty's favorite textile designers.

PART OF THE ATTRACTION OF PETER GETTY'S handsome, mansard-roofed residence in Pacific Heights has always been its rich history and musical connections.

Getty, a Harvard graduate, musician, and accomplished art collector (he presciently acquired a large work by Basquiat when the young artist was still alive), liked the low-key location and admired the design of the house. It has been designated a San Francisco historic landmark.

Influenced by the Second Empire style of French architecture popular in the 1870s, the residence, surrounded by a rose-scented garden, has been called Victorian, baroque, and Italianate in style. Painted all white, it is a handsome example of the period, with an asymmetrical form, a center entry up a flight of stairs, and a charming variety of ornate windows, conservatories, and cornices.

The rich history of the house began with the fourteen-year-old Leander S. Sherman, who left his native Boston by steamer and arrived in San Francisco in 1861. He swept downtown sidewalks and assisted in a small music shop. By 1870 he was able to buy the business.

In 1876 Sherman purchased a lot in a lovely, rustic neighborhood called Cow Hollow. Sherman paid $5,000 cash for the highly desirable site, set on a low hill and offering expansive bay views. He and his wife built a family home, which they used to entertain musicians visiting the city. The pretty chanteuse, Lotta Crabtree, as well as Ignacy Jan Paderewski, the Polish violinist, performed in the music room (where Getty performs concerts for his friends and family today). The Sherman daughters, Claire and Elsie, were pianists, joining the celebrated guests and delighting their proud parents.

Glamorous evenings at the Sherman house became part of the city's society legend.

Following the Shermans' deaths, the house became a dancing school. Its nineteen rooms and Victorian-style garden and carriage house served as a decorator showcase, and then were converted into an elegant private hotel.

Now, thanks to Peter Getty and his friends, the music has returned.

ONE OF A PAIR OF RARE SEVENTEENTH-CENTURY EMBROIDERED AND APPLIQUÉD SILK pastoral panels hangs on the wall of the music room of the Sherman House. Originally from a *hôtel particulier* on the Place Beauvau in Paris, they were removed in 1970 and later acquired by Ann Getty. Two of the four ormolu wall lights in the music room are of the Louis XVI period, and the others are in the style of Louis XVI. The quartet of armchairs, including the one above, is second-quarter eighteenth-century *Regence*, in giltwood and tapestry. The Gobelins tapestries depict scenes from the Fables of La Fontaine and are from the collection of Florence J. Gould, Sotheby's, Monaco. The George III bronze-mounted, black-japanned cabinet in the manner of Pierre Langlois is circa 1760.

THE SITTING ROOM IS HOME TO MIXED-MEDIA PAINTINGS by Claes Oldenburg (upper right), Robert Motherwell (left), and Robert Rauschenberg (lower right). The Oldenburg piece, 1963, was acquired from a sale of the estate of Robert and Ethel Scull. A pair of George III giltwood armchairs, attributed to the Ince and Mayhew furniture workshop, has fluted, tapering legs and gadrooned pinched feet. *Opposite:* The George II parcel-gilt carved wood pier mirror with ribbon-tied flowers centered at the top was in the collection of Ronald and Nancy Tree, Ditchley Park, Oxford (where the pair hung in the drawing room), and later of Marietta Tree. Beneath the mirror is a Louis XIV ormolu-mounted painted strong box, circa 1700.

THE DINING ROOM WAS DECORATED BY ANN GETTY in an understated style, with muted colors. On the wall hangs an oil-on-canvas painting, *A Painter and His Model* by Pablo Picasso, circa 1963. Sets of sixteen mahogany and part-ebonized dining chairs, circa 1815, have also been reproduced in the Ann Getty House collection. The late-eighteenth-century Northern European ormolu and cut-glass six-light chandelier has an umbrella-shaped canopy. The angular candle branches are hung with cut-glass ropes and prisms.

PETER GETTY'S STUDY IS OFTEN USED AS A DINING ROOM for a small group. *Above:* A series of six hand-painted Flora Danica porcelain plates, by Royal Copenhagen, are accompanied by a French service in silver, parcel-gilt, and agate. The stem is formed as trailing grapevines with a salamander on each side. The silver is Paris, 1840, with maker's marks Maurice Mayer and Pierre-Francois Queille. *Opposite and above:* A collection of twenty hand-painted plaster scientific mushrooms, toadstools, and fungi specimens, each with a label in Latin, are late nineteenth-century German.

IN THE LIBRARY, WHICH HOUSES PETER GETTY'S COLLECTION OF RARE BOOKS, is a pair of Italian Renaissance marble-inset giltwood mirrors, late sixteenth century. Each mirror has a mirror plate flanked by figural pilasters and surmounted by a foliate scrolling panel.

THE ITALIAN TERRESTRIAL LIBRARY GLOBE, circa 1688, was made by Vincenzo Coronelli (1650–1718). The hand-colored globe is set in a Dutch-style stand with four turned, ebonized legs with gilt-painted bands. The same legs inspired the placement and design of the surrounding bookcase. Casework in the library was designed by Ed McEachron and crafted by Phoenix Woodworking. *Above*: A sofa is upholstered in commissioned Luigi Bevilacqua silk velvet, selected in Venice by senior designer Maria Quiros, a textiles specialist. On the wall above the sofa hangs a pair of Basil Besler circa-1613 hand-colored copperplate engravings.

HAND-PAINTED SILK VELVET COVERS THE BED in a north-facing guest bedroom with superb views over the sheltered garden and San Francisco Bay beyond. Beside the bed is a late-nineteenth-century Russian simulated-tortoiseshell lamp with brass and gilt metal mounts, on an octagonal base. It was acquired through Mallett, London. The mid-nineteenth-century green-stained horn chair with saber legs was designed with a Turkish influence.

A VERY RARE, IRON-MOUNTED, TWO-PART MEXICAN CABINET, 1740, is crafted of ebony, bone, etched ivory, fruitwood, and satinwood. It's one of a small group of similar cabinets made in Puebla, Mexico. The others are in museums in Mexico. The bureau opens to reveal small drawers, niches, and pigeonholes, as well as elaborate inlays of marquetry and an inscribed map. (A close-up detail of the etched ivory and rare wood inlay is on page 82.)

ANN GETTY WANTS TO MAKE HER GUESTS VERY WELCOME. She lavishes guest rooms with draped antique beds and provides desks, cabinets, book-cases, and delightful chairs for their comfort—in her own residences and in this bedroom she designed for her son, Peter Getty. *Opposite:* A pair of George III painted wheel-back armchairs, circa 1780, was originally acquired from Gerald Spyer & Son, London, by Parish-Hadley. The contemporary Amboyna burl–veneer writing table with twenty-two-karat gilding on the acanthus leaf details was crafted by Rossi Antiques for the Ann Getty House collection. *Above:* A 1980 gouache on paper by David Hockney hangs above the Leavitt Weaver upholstered headboard.

IN THE RED GUEST BEDROOM IS A GEORGE III MAHOGANY FOUR-POSTER BED, made by Wright and Elwick for Tabley House in Cheshire. (Tabley House was designed by John Carr of York for Sir Peter Byrne Leicester, Bt., and completed in 1769. J.M.W. Turner was among the British artists who painted there.) The scroll-carved, pierced cornice is covered in silk fabric. The contemporary chair, modeled after an antique in the Getty collection, is from the Ann Getty House collection. Between the windows is a George II mahogany and parcel-gilt chest on stand, circa 1755. The paneled sides have carrying handles.

A CONTEMPORARY TUFTED SOFA MADE BY HILDE-BRAND FURNITURE IS BASED ON THE "BRANCH" SETTEE originally designed by Elsie de Wolfe. The white-velvet-upholstered chairs were also custom-made by Hilde-Brand Furniture, based on the de Wolfe design. The hand-carved bases with metal tree branches were created by Campero, San Francisco. The pair of white-painted stools on twisted tree-form supports, circa 1930, was made by Jansen of Paris, 1930.

CHAPTER THREE

The Temple of Wings
Berkeley Hills, California

THE TEMPLE OF WINGS, VIEWED FROM THE DRIVEWAY, is open to the Western sun and views across beautifully wooded Berkeley hillsides. Bernard Maybeck is generally credited with the design (though he had a falling out with his client, Florence Treadwell Boynton, and the young architect Randolph Monro supervised the construction in 1914). Maybeck's classical architecture background, close friendship with the Boynton family (he lived nearby), lofty ideals, and love of classicism inspired and fueled the design of a pair of sheltering wings surmounting a peristyle of thirty-four Corinthian columns, cast in concrete in place. Originally open to the elements, it was rebuilt after a 1924 wildfire and the enclosed wings were added, along with a miniscule kitchen excavated into the hillside. Paint colors are authentic to this period.

WITH ITS DAZZLING COLLECTION OF ESOTERIC
and rare Aesthetic Movement treasures, the 1911–14 Temple of
Wings is like a trip into the fevered minds and imaginations of the
period's philosophical painters and craftsmen and its finest gilders,
glassmakers, and cabinetmakers. Hidden on a eucalyptus-clad hillside, the temple includes virtuoso examples of this unabashed cult
of beauty, all emphasizing the primacy of artistic expression.

The interiors and their highly focused objects and paintings
were assembled by Ann Getty with her son, John Getty, a musician and songwriter. His devotion to each museum-worthy piece
in this project and her attention to decorative details have resulted
in rooms of poetic beauty and astonishing quality.

The rooms in this romantic landmark residence—discreet,
graceful, and coherent—demonstrate Getty's passion for research, her distinctive taste, and her innate ability to create harmonious room decor from daring, disparate, and often eccentric

pieces found around the world. Each corner is superbly arranged
with vignettes and the finest examples of intriguing artistry, including Persian-inspired William de Morgan pottery, accompanied by an exquisitely rendered 1879 Jules Bastien-Lepage portrait of Sarah Bernhardt.

Placed near a Tiffany Studios "Wisteria" lamp, with its gleaming rivulets of blue glass, are Daum Nancy opalescent glass Art
Nouveau vases, 1910; an Emile Gallé gold cameo vase depicting
thistles in violet and periwinkle; and an opaque pale amber Gallé
cameo vase, 1900, its swirls of turquoise and brown glass depicting
marine life and fronds of seaweed.

The living room of the Temple of Wings (formerly known as
the Temple of the Winds) offers a connoisseur's eye on the highest
ideals of collecting, and celebrates—even venerates—the Victorian avant-garde (1860–1900) and its later coteries and American
disciples like the artists of Tiffany Studios.

THE WALLS OF THE LIVING ROOM AT THE TEMPLE OF WINGS are painted a moody and mutable tone that looks like blue/teal in the early morning light and darkens in the afternoon and twilight hours to peacock blue, a favorite color of William Morris. In the spirit of early-twentieth-century bohemian Berkeley, a time of high ideals and worldly cultural exploration, Ann Getty orchestrated a collection of museum-worthy Arts and Crafts furniture, paintings, pottery, Tiffany lamps, carpets, and paintings. Highlights include (in the foreground) a circa-1840 ivory and ebony octagonal table with legs turned in the neo-Renaissance style, topped with a Tiffany "Dragonfly" lamp. A walnut, ivory, and brass table, right, is nineteenth-century Italian. Paintings include *The Bath of Psyche* by Lord Frederick Leighton (second from right).

IN EVERY CORNER OF THE LIVING ROOM, the subtle and atmospheric lighting favored by Ann Getty is augmented with reflective Favrile glass objects, carved silver picture frames, and opalescent Daum glass vases. *Left:* A dramatic collection of late-nineteenth-century glazed William de Morgan rice dishes and bowls, in the Persian manner, was designed by Charles Passenger (marked C.P.). *Opposite:* A Jessie Bayes cabinet, circa 1910, was made by F. Beattie. The intricate gilded and painted cabinet is decorated with quotations from Sir Thomas Mallory's *Le Morte d'Arthur*, along with imagery inspired by the romantic Arthurian legends and characters. The pair of Egyptian-revival footstools was crafted in the early twentieth century. The 1879 portrait of Sarah Bernhardt painted by Jules Bastien-Lepage is a recent favorite of international museum curators and has been included in definitive exhibitions on the artist at the Musée d'Orsay in Paris, the Royal Academy in London, and the California Palace of the Legion of Honor in San Francisco.

Elaborate furniture celebrating the Arthurian myths, Greek legends, neo-Gothic taste, and reverence for nature achieves a harmony between art and history as Getty brings them together with textiles, furniture of historical importance, and paintings by leading practitioners of the time.

There is a rare Tiffany "Dragonfly" lamp, with shimmering insect wings in delicate striated opalescent glass, and a dreamy 1895 gold-framed painting, *A Coign of Vantage* by Sir Lawrence Alma-Tadema, hovering above a graceful Victorian ebonized and upholstered occasional chair. A bravura painting, *Le Printemps* by William-Adolphe Bouguereau, 1858, first exhibited in the Paris Salon of 1857, hangs above a superbly crafted Herter Brothers Ottoman and Japanese-inspired lacquer and gilt-bronze cabinet, 1880, originally commissioned for the Astor family.

In the study, a privately commissioned, ornately carved Herter Brothers library table, 1878, is topped with a vivid collection of Tiffany and Lalique vases, as well as Tiffany Studios lamps and a seventeen-piece Tiffany Studios gilt-bronze desk set in the Pine-needle pattern.

The house has a romantic story. The Temple of Wings, now a landmark and tribute to the bohemian early twentieth century in Berkeley, was originally designed by Bernard Maybeck in 1911–14 as a residence and studio for dance teacher Florence Treadwell Boynton, her husband Charles, and their seven children. For Maybeck, influenced by the utopian ideals of John Ruskin and William Morris, the perfect California house was the native California landscape, with just a few buildings scattered around "in case of rain."

AN 1828 GEORGE IV BURR ELM BREAKFAST TABLE, crafted by George Humble of Kelso and designed by John Dobson, makes a handsome platform for a series of Daum and Gallé vases and bowls, and a collection of Tiffany Studios Favrile glass and bronze jeweled candlesticks in the Moorish style, circa 1910.

A classically trained architect, Maybeck contributed the concept of a simple central Greek temple–inspired structure supported on a series of Corinthian columns. Determined to respect the topography and build artistic houses that appeared to have grown out of the hillside, Maybeck, a proponent of establishing Berkeley as an "Athens of the West," sited the Temple of Wings among native oak and eucalyptus trees on a hillside plot.

There the Boynton family planned their ideal of "the simple life," with ancient Greece–inspired furniture and plaster casts of Greek statuary (some granted a look of authenticity by missing limbs and a patina of Berkeley dust). Florence Boynton was a devotee of Isadora Duncan (a childhood friend), and the temple became the site of dancers in floating togas striking poses in a terpsichorean fantasy. The temple had no walls, but rain and storms were kept at bay by romantic linen curtains that drifted in the breeze. There was no kitchen. Vegetarians, the Boyntons lived on California fruits, cheese, honey, milk, and roasted peanuts.

The structure that for some years was designated "The Temple of the Winds," was destroyed in the Berkeley wildfire of 1924. Eventually it was rebuilt as a more conventional residence with walls, the columns incorporated into the enclosure.

The Boynton children lived there into the 1980s, and daughter Sulgwyn Boynton taught Greek-inspired dance to young girls in flowing garments amid the columns of the Temple of Wings.

The temple was acquired in the 1990s by musician/songwriter John Getty, the son of Gordon and Ann Getty.

THE HANDSOME "WISTERIA" TABLE LAMP BY TIFFANY STUDIOS, circa 1905–10, was designed by Clara Driscoll and crafted of leaded glass and patinated bronze. Illuminated in the evening, it glimmers with intricate shades of blue, mauve, and green, in harmony with the William Morris fabric curtains and the exquisite oil painting *A Coign of Vantage* by the Dutch-British artist Sir Lawrence Alma-Tadema (1836–1912). A favorite of museum curators, the painting has been exhibited at the Metropolitan Museum of Art in New York, among others. The octagonal Bugatti table, circa 1900, is crafted with ebony and parchment decoration. *Above:* An oil-on-canvas painting, *Le Printemps*, 1858, is by the French painter William-Adolphe Bouguereau. *Overleaf:* In the study, a collection of Tiffany Studios lamps stands on a Herter Brothers American Aesthetic carved walnut library table, 1878. A pair of paintings of dancing girls in swirling robes, by Lord Frederick Leighton, 1869, hangs between the windows.

ON A NEO-GOTHIC TABLE IN THE LIBRARY is a selection of Arts and Crafts pottery, *opposite*, including pieces by Grueby Faience Company and Newcomb College Pottery. On the gilded leather-topped Herter Brothers library desk, *above*, is a collection of Tiffany Studios gold Aurene glass objects, 1900.

THE SKYLIT BATHROOM IN THE TEMPLE OF WINGS is centered upon a bath framed in handmade tiles, with a Tiffany stained-glass window. On the mantel, surrounded by rare glass pieces, stands an oil painting from 1900 by the British artist Frederick Marriott. Among the glittering array of decorative vases and bowls are an Emile Gallé circa-1900 "blow-out" aquatic vase, a Muller Frères Lunéville 1910 cameo vase, a Gabriel Argy-Rousseau 1924 bowl with clusters of star-shaped creatures in *pâte de verre*, and a wheel-carved and etched glass vase, 1890, by Ernest Baptist Reveillé, with underwater scenes and writhing fish.

CHAPTER FOUR

A House in the Sacramento Valley

THE GILBERT FAMILY RESIDENCE WHERE ANN GETTY GREW up has the snow-smudged Sierra foothills as a backdrop and miles of walnut orchards in the soft, green foreground. The central building, designed by architect Tom Potts, is original, and a pool house/guesthouse, outbuildings, and graceful loggias were added in later years.

Ann Getty observed that the valley is intersected by rivers, sloughs, and creeks fed by snow runoff, including Grasshopper Slough, Dry Creek, and the nearby Bear River (Rio Oso in Spanish). The sloughs are filled with small fish, turtles, and frogs, and dense willows and mossy banks are home to dragonflies.

It is an idyllic region, and Ann and her beloved brothers would play and swim in the rivers as children. She recalled digging and searching for flint and obsidian Indian arrowheads, which are common in the area.

In the spring, wisteria crowns the gateway leading from the walnut orchards to the side entrance of the house. The glazed Anduze pots are from Provence.

BROAD LOGGIAS WERE ADDED TO THE HOUSE (taking traditional Spanish cloisters as inspiration) to offer shelter from the intense Sacramento Valley heat in summer. They also provide a cool spot for a late-afternoon aperitif or quiet reading. Wisteria vines planted throughout the garden thrive through the cold winters and very hot summers.

ANYONE CRISSCROSSING THE FLAT AGRICULTURAL land of the northern Sacramento Valley might be surprised to find Ann Getty.

Getty, who directs her design firm in San Francisco and explores the world for the finest art and antiques, is at heart, she says, a farmer.

Her father acquired walnut and peach orchards outside the small agricultural town of Wheatland in Northern California. Ann Gilbert and her two brothers grew up in this fertile farmland near the Sacramento River. Members of her family still farm in the region. And it is here in Yuba County that Ann rode her bicycle along quiet roads and would take her horse to the river to join her brothers for a swim.

"Our life was very healthy and carefree," recalled Getty. And even today the country house is her retreat. But in a recent remodel, she did not forget her love of baroque splendor.

The formal rooms showcase her favorite antiques, several of them originally purchased from Sister Parish of Parish-Hadley. Tufted sofas and chairs shimmer with hand-woven silks, banquettes are lavished with tiger-striped Bevilacqua velvets, and pillows gleam with gold-threaded antique tapestries. It's exotic and dazzling, yet comfortable.

Bedrooms in Wheatland are bewitching. An Anglo-Indian guest suite with portraits of maharajahs and desks inlaid with mother-of-pearl beside carved bamboo beds feels like a retreat in a Jodhpur palace.

After a day of swimming or an evening of bowling, guests and grandchildren can often be found sprawled on silken sofas. Friends curl up to sip champagne on chairs covered with luscious hand-woven Venetian silk velvets and antique Lyon silk brocade fragments.

A series of antique Chinese porcelain Buddhist saint figures, each delicately detailed and colored, stands on a carved and gilded tree of life that is mounted on a gilded lacquer chinoiserie panel on a wall in the living room.

The dining room has a museum-like trove of Dutch masters and a spectacular Baccarat chandelier dripping with cut-glass baubles and faceted crystal. Embroidered silk cascades about a carved and gilded antique four-poster bed in the "Blue" guest room.

"Beauty can be so uplifting," said Getty. "I cherish the antiques and paintings in my country house. They were crafted as long ago as 1673, and as far away as Holland, China, Portuguese Goa and India, England, and France, and they all have fascinating stories."

ROSE ARBORS, MOSSY PATHWAYS, STATUARY, fountains, decorative gates, and antique stone urns punctuate the walled garden. The house and garden are truly private, with high, creeper-covered walls around the periphery, and the inner garden, right, is a scented haven for birds and the Gettys' young grandchildren. Elsewhere are a croquet lawn, tennis court, pool, and bowling alley, as well as bicycling along endless flat country roads with only darting birds and the occasional beaten-up farm truck to break the silence.

ONE EARLY SPRING, JUST AS THE CHERRY BLOSSOMS WERE IN FULL BLOOM, an unexpected storm swirled in from the Sierra and turned the tender flowers into pink "snow." It was a surreal sight when guests strolled in the garden the following morning. A pair of chairs is positioned outside the doors to the living room.

THE LIVING ROOM WALLS ARE COVERED with eight English chinoiserie panels, circa 1740. Getty has embellished them with a pair of George II tree-form wall sconces, circa 1760, with Chinese porcelain figures. Subtle but atmospheric, the walls and interior architectural details were hand-painted by Russell and Boals, Yuba County, with delicate oak-veined and gilded faux-bois details. Above the mantel hangs a circa-1760 George III giltwood mirror from Parish-Hadley.

THE CURTAINS IN THE LIVING ROOM, IN THE BISHOP-SLEEVE STYLE, ARE CRAFTED IN THREE
shades of Indian silk, *opposite*. A pair of George I gilded armchairs covered in antique blue damask were originally
from Spye Park House, a historic Palladian mansion near Bath. The corner banquettes, made by Hilde-Brand, San
Francisco, are covered in custom-woven tiger-stripe silk velvet by Bevilacqua, Venice. The extremely rare carpet was
woven in Lahore, India, circa 1830.

THE CIRCA-1760 SOLID EBONY ENGLISH BOOKCASE, with sixty exquisite Chinese mirror paintings on the doors, might offer a secret insight to Ann Getty's taste. "It would be very difficult to choose, but if I was to pick my favorite piece of furniture, it would be this George II breakfront cabinet," she said. "It is not the most important piece, but I think it is the most beautiful. I love the way the glass mirror paintings shimmer and catch the light. Chinoiserie is one of my favorite styles, and this is a wonderful example." The bookcase is from the Marquis of Milford Haven, Moyns Park, Essex, UK. The chandelier is by Baccarat, early twentieth century. Surrounding the late-nineteenth-century mahogany dining table are sixteen circa-1720 Anglo-Dutch chairs in the style of Daniel Marot with Dutch baroque curves and elaborate fish-scale patterns. (Getty's mother's family was Dutch.) Included is a pair of almost-matching Dutch baroque chairs and eight custom-carved reproductions by Agrell Architectural Carving, Mill Valley, California. On the table are early Regency-period cut-glass and twin-branch candelabra, circa 1805.

TO BALANCE THE ENCHANTMENT OF THE MIRRORED CABINET on the opposite wall of the dining room, Ann Getty hung an array of rare Dutch Old Master paintings, including, center, a still life with apples, and, lower right, an overturned basket with fruit, both mid-seventeenth century, by Balthasar Van Der Ast. Other pieces include a Delftware bowl and fruit painting, middle right, by David de Heem, and wild strawberries in a Delftware bowl by Jacob van Hulsdonck, both mid-seventeenth century.

ON ONE SIDE OF THE KITCHEN (which is not in period style) is a cozy Dutch-style corner with a series of Delftware and famille rose Chinese export plates on the wall. Two early-eighteenth-century Queen Anne armchairs are upholstered in gros point and petit point depicting exotic birds and chinoiserie figures. The late-nineteenth-century painting is by Lady Laura Theresa Alma-Tadema, the wife of Sir Lawrence Alma-Tadema (whose painting hangs at John Getty's Temple of Wings in Berkeley). Lady Laura specialized in paintings depicting seventeenth-century settings like this example.

IN THE STAIRWAY LEADING TO THE UPSTAIRS BEDROOMS, a wall was decorated with delicate Chinese motifs and landscapes, with traditional court figures, commissioned in the seventies by Ann Getty and supervised by the late designer Eleanor Ford. Getty asked the artist, now unknown, to include peaches and walnuts (her crops) into the allegory of seasons and country life.

The Regency brass and mahogany birdcage (on a later stand) was crafted in the early nineteenth century. The circular cage has a pierced tapering roof and trellised cupola with an eagle finial. On the rectangular base, supported by foliate volutes, are plaques of goddesses in peacock-drawn chariots. It's an inspiring piece to pass each morning and evening.

THE BLUE BEDROOM AT ANN GETTY'S COUNTRY HOUSE IS ONE OF HER favorite rooms, and she often changes the paintings and furniture here. It's a canvas for design experimentation and adding new pieces. Side tables from the early nineteenth century were from the Paris collection of Mr. and Mrs. Gustav Herman Kinnicutt (the parents of Sister Parish, from whom these were acquired). The tables are offset by the rosy splendor of the Nicholas I Russian tapestry rug, circa 1835, from the 1983 Luttrellstown Castle sale. The pair of painted and parcel-gilt Regency armchairs, circa 1800, has been attributed to Thomas Hope, a prodigiously talented English decorator, author of design books, and tastemaker of the period, who undertook several Grand Tours of Europe when he was barely twenty. He returned and decorated his house in London with lavish and elaborate furnishings inspired by his travels. These chairs are possibly from that Cavendish Square residence.

IN THE BLUE BEDROOM IS A LATE-EIGHTEENTH-CENTURY PAINTED AND parcel-gilt George III four-poster bed, dressed in embroidered silks from Old World Weavers. The pale blue silk is from Silk Trading Company. Ann Getty is very fond of large-scale eighteenth-century chairs, particularly this pair of painted and gilded scroll-arm Regency chairs, attributed to Thomas Hope. They are upholstered in fragments of silk brocade, circa 1780, woven in Lyon.

ON THE DRESSING TABLE, also draped in embroidered silk, stands an 1800 Russian table mirror crafted in walrus ivory and mother-of-pearl, *above*. The circa-1780 painted and gilded chair, with carving in the manner of Thomas Chippendale, is one of a set of four.

THE "BAMBOO" GUEST BEDROOM, HIDDEN
IN A CORNER OF A WING OF THE HOUSE,
is a fascinating retreat that reflects Ann Getty's en-
during love for traditional Indian decorative arts and
Anglo-Indian craftsmanship. Front and center is a fine
example of the art of Mughal India, a nineteenth-
century painted padouk wood chest that depicts sari-
clad women and peacocks in palace gardens. Walls are
covered with Rosemount cotton by Marvic, London.

IN THE BAMBOO GUEST BEDROOM, WHICH OVERLOOKS THE GARDEN, the nineteenth-century faux-bamboo beds inspired the room's door surrounds, trim, and crown molding. In a colorful row above the twin beds, the mid-nineteenth-century Indian portraits are reverse painting on glass (*verre eglomisé*). The rug is a rare nineteenth-century Louis Phillippe needlepoint, circa 1840, acquired in London. The nineteenth-century Chinese export bamboo chairs, *opposite,* with added steel underpinnings, have great intricacy, charm, and fragility. On the table at right is an early-nineteenth-century English whalebone and copper Russian-style stepped box with mica underlay. The eighteenth-century tortoiseshell and ivory table cabinet is from Portuguese Goa. The traveling desk, from the early nineteenth century, is crafted in sandalwood and metal-inlaid ivory.

IN THIS ALLURING GUEST BEDROOM IS A ROCOCO REVIVAL PAINTED AND GILDED POTTERY CHIMNEYPIECE, circa 1840. On the mantel is a George III ormolu white marble Temple clock by Vulliamy with a Derby biscuit figure of a woman, acquired from the Prince of Wales in 1811 and purchased from Hotspur, London. The crystal candlesticks are Victorian, and the Louis XV giltwood carved mirror over the mantelpiece was acquired from Sotheby's.

In this bedroom, with views over the walnut groves, a fine needlepoint carpet emphasizes the theme of roses that animates the decor. The late-nineteenth-century gros-point carpet with ebullient patterns of roses is French. Two Napoleon III–style chintz-upholstered gilt rope-twist chairs are late–nineteenth-century reproductions. Below the gilt mirror, right, is a superb-quality eighteenth-century English blanket chest, circa 1865, in black and gold lacquer, from the estate of Nancy Lancaster.

THE LATE-NINETEENTH-CENTURY FRENCH OPALINE TODDY SET painted with birds and flowers consists of a tray, goblets, a decanter, and a sucrier. It is finely hand-painted with gilt arches and borders. The garden—with its arbors of roses and jasmine, and parterres of poppies, lavender, and peonies—provides fragrant fresh-cut flowers. The glazed ceramic circa-1840 fireplace, *opposite*, is ornamented with exotic birds and foliage.

JACQUES-EMILE BLANCHE (1861–1942) painted *Petite Fille aux Hortensias* in Varengeville, on the Normandy coast. The region was also a favorite of Monet and Braque. The painted commode, circa 1775, is attributed to cabinetmaker George Brookshaw. In the George III style, it has a gilt-painted center panel flanked by cupboards. The commode was reputedly supplied to Sir Hugh Percy, the Duke of Cumberland, who was a major patron of Canaletto. At center, the copper, mica, and whalebone stepped box, late eighteenth century, is Russian. The two ivory and shagreen tea caddies, with ball finials, are Continental, from the early nineteenth century. The Regency penwork-decorated worktable, *opposite*, is detailed with period figures and floral sprays.

A DUTCH BAROQUE JAPANNED OAK LINEN PRESS FROM THE SECOND QUARTER OF THE EIGHTEENTH CENTURY has a concave cornice, a pair of paneled doors, and a frieze of drawers. It is set on a bombé case with four drawers and bronze hardware and stands a noble eight feet high. An exquisite piece, it is decorated with watery architectural and figural scenes in tones of gold, with animated raised gilt figures on a *tête-de-nègre* ground. The Napoleon III–style giltwood rope twist chair, *above*, has an arched backrest and a virtuoso knotted top rail.

ANN GILBERT GETTY'S FAMILY STILL FARMS WALNUT ORCHARDS IN THIS REMOTE CORNER OF YUBA COUNTY. The property, *overleaf*, is home to robins, bluebirds, woodpeckers, hummingbirds, owls, egrets, Swenson hawks, peregrine falcons, and abundant migrating waterfowl. Getty loves spring, when cherry blossoms and wisteria bloom, and she also likes the fulfillment of fall—the excitement, hard work, and long hours of the walnut harvest. Warm summer nights are dramatic with thunderstorms and lightning in the Sierra, and stars are especially bright because there are no city lights to dull the star-scattered sky.

CHAPTER FIVE

F. Scott and Terry Gross House
Nob Hill, San Francisco

WHEN SAN FRANCISCO ANTIQUE DEALER AND philanthropist Terry Gross and her husband, Scott, acquired their classical 1920s apartment on the crest of Nob Hill in San Francisco, she knew exactly how she would decorate and embellish the rooms. On buying trips to Paris over the last decades, she acquired exquisite furniture from top French antique dealers. They often invited her to visit the private studios of decorative artists, along with workshops of torchbearers of arcane techniques, and by-appointment-only top antique restorers.

When Gross visited the atmospheric headquarters of Féau & Cie, with treasure troves of centuries-old boiseries and dusty, dismantled carved and gilded antique rooms, she was seduced by the beauty, spirit, and allegorical artistry.

At the fabled Atelier de Ricou, hidden on a leafy street just beyond the Paris Périphérique, she watched decorative artists creating poetic effects with raw-earth pigments, gold leaf, and old-world artists' recipes (rabbit-skin glue, among others) to conjure up worlds of the imagination.

These insider sources became the key to her dream of a Continental salon for her San Francisco decor. She signed up architect Thomas Kligerman and Scott & Warner Builders, San Francisco, to rearrange and improve proportions of the rooms and make elegant sense of the layout.

Gross commissioned the Ricou team to create large-scale Tiepolo-esque murals of vivid fantasy Chinese scenes for the paneled dining room.

Féau & Cie were complicit in giving the apartment the trappings of a Paris *hôtel particulier*, with superb carved and gilded paneling for the walls, and a hall of mirrors with *Regence*-style palm moldings. The company's painstaking specialists took up residence at the apartment, finishing, installing antique mirrors, and perfecting discreet painted effects. Even the window and door hardware is French, crafted using late-eighteenth-century techniques by the venerable Bricard Company.

"I wanted to create a synthesis of traditional European styles, with my favorite antiques from France, Italy, and Belgium," said Gross. "All of the best pieces from all periods work here in harmony."

As the work progressed, Gross found a kindred spirit in Ann Getty, consulting with her on textiles for the apartment, acquiring eight of her chinoiserie Badminton chairs, and adding crystal and coral objets d'art from Getty's personal collection.

"Ann suggested an oval dining table for eight so that the conversation could be enjoyed by everyone," said Gross.

The pair continued a dialogue that enriched the decor and brought layers of textiles and subtle decoration to give the rooms added luster.

"When you're working with Ann, you have access to specialist textile artists, to top talents," said Gross. "As a designer she never pushed me to her personal taste. She has great style but she was open to my concepts. She listens and then she interprets and makes your ideas better than you could dream. It was a very inspiring experience."

To enhance the chinoiserie in the dining room, Getty sent a precious Chippendale cabinet from her collection to her favorite carving studio in Los Angeles to be copied. The result is a one-of-a-kind piece, authentic in every detail to the spirit of Chippendale.

Now the apartment is the background for fund-raisers for Terry's garden club and events for the Institute of Classical Architecture and Art, as well as San Francisco art museums. Her vision was realized.

Few interiors in San Francisco are as lovely, as exquisitely created.

TERRY GROSS PLANNED THE ELABORATE MIRRORED HALLWAY OF HER Nob Hill apartment, *previous pages*, as a subtle homage to the Hall of Mirrors, the dazzling feature of the Château de Versailles. It is also a nod to California interior designer Frances Elkins, another Francophile, who first introduced the chic plaster palmier columns and torchères of 1920s Paris designer Serge Roche to her clients. These hallway moldings were created in white plaster from original *Regence* models by Féau & Cie. The company, founded in 1875, specializes in paneling and moldings, both historic and newly created. Eighteenth- and nineteenth-century mercury glass mirrors were installed by French specialists who had recently worked on restorations at the Château de Versailles. On the eighteenth-century gilt brackets, from the Craig Wright collection, a series of silver goblets holds simple pinecones painted with matte white paint.

ANN GETTY CONSULTED WITH TERRY GROSS regarding textiles, curtains, decor, and furniture for the apartment, including the sumptuous but sedate living room. Creating a versatile conversation grouping near the south-facing windows are a pair of Schiaparelli-style curved sofas from Michael Taylor Designs accompanied by gilt Louis XV–style chairs. The pale celadon and taupe carpet is an Oushak.

THE CURVES OF THE GRACEFUL ANTIQUE FRENCH FRAME seem to mirror the silhouette of the odalisque in the Matisse lithograph from the mid-1920s, *above*. Matisse lovers admire the way the artist created an authentic Moroccan harem setting in his Nice studio with Marrakesh textiles, atmospheric props, and carpets, as backdrops for his favorite model, actress Henriette Darricarrère, a young ballet dancer and musician. *Opposite*: Gross created her own gracefully powerful vignette with a nineteenth-century albino loggerhead turtle carapace, a polychrome Tang dynasty figure, and antique breastplate necklaces from Oceania, acquired in Antwerp. Delicate golden ornamentation includes Italian tole and iron sconces, and a water-gilded *Regence* mirror reflected in the eighteenth-century French giltwood mirror.

THE DINING ROOM DECOR IS ANIMATED
BY EIGHT BADMINTON CHAIRS from the
Ann Getty House collection. Copies of the legendary chinoiserie chairs from Badminton House,
these chairs are upholstered in embroidered silk
that Getty commissioned from one of her favorite
Chinese studios. The Getty family has two of the
original de-accessioned Badminton House chairs
(acquired at auction in the 1980s), and another pair
is on display at London's Victoria & Albert Museum. A promenade of Tiepolo-style murals portray-
ing elaborate Chinese *magot* figures marries Italian
romantic dreams of exoticism with the passion for
chinoiserie of Getty and Gross. The colorful murals were painted by artists from Atelier de Ricou,
Paris, in homage to the magnificent 1757 wall decor
at Palladio's Villa Valmarana ai Nani, painted by Gi-
andomenico Tiepolo, the son of Gianbattista.

SHIMMERING GOLD-EMBELLISHED RED JAPANNED FINISHES transformed the apartment's retiring room into a ravishing experience. The complex japanning finishes—originally European imitations of traditional multilayered Chinese and Japanese lacquer finishes—were crafted in San Francisco by Warner Graves and Eric Ismay. The in-demand duo of Ismay and Graves are master artists specializing in eighteenth-century restorations and decorative painting, and in particular japanning techniques. Intricate panels were drawn and planned by the apartment's architect, Thomas Kligerman of Ike Kligerman Barkley Architects, with offices in San Francisco and New York. Entering the reverie-inducing red-on-red suite (an ultra-luxe powder room with a sumptuous cinnabar silk velvet banquette), guests encounter a carved giltwood chinoiserie mirror and gilt sconces hovering above a red lacquer bombé chest.

IN SCOTT GROSS'S DRESSING ROOM, *overleaf,* a spectacular example of an antique Italian grotto chair with a gleaming nacreous shell back and pearl-encrusted legs takes pride of place. Its writhing sea creatures, so vividly carved and authentically grotesque, appear ready to come alive and plunge forward. The shagreen finish and paneling were painted by San Francisco decorative artist Willem Racké. Terry Gross commissioned superbly gilded moldings (by Féau & Cie) and jewel-like window hardware from Bricard, a French company founded in 1782 that made locks and hardware for Louis XVI. Each piece was cast, carved, gold-plated, chiseled, and assembled by hand in Bricard's Paris workshops.

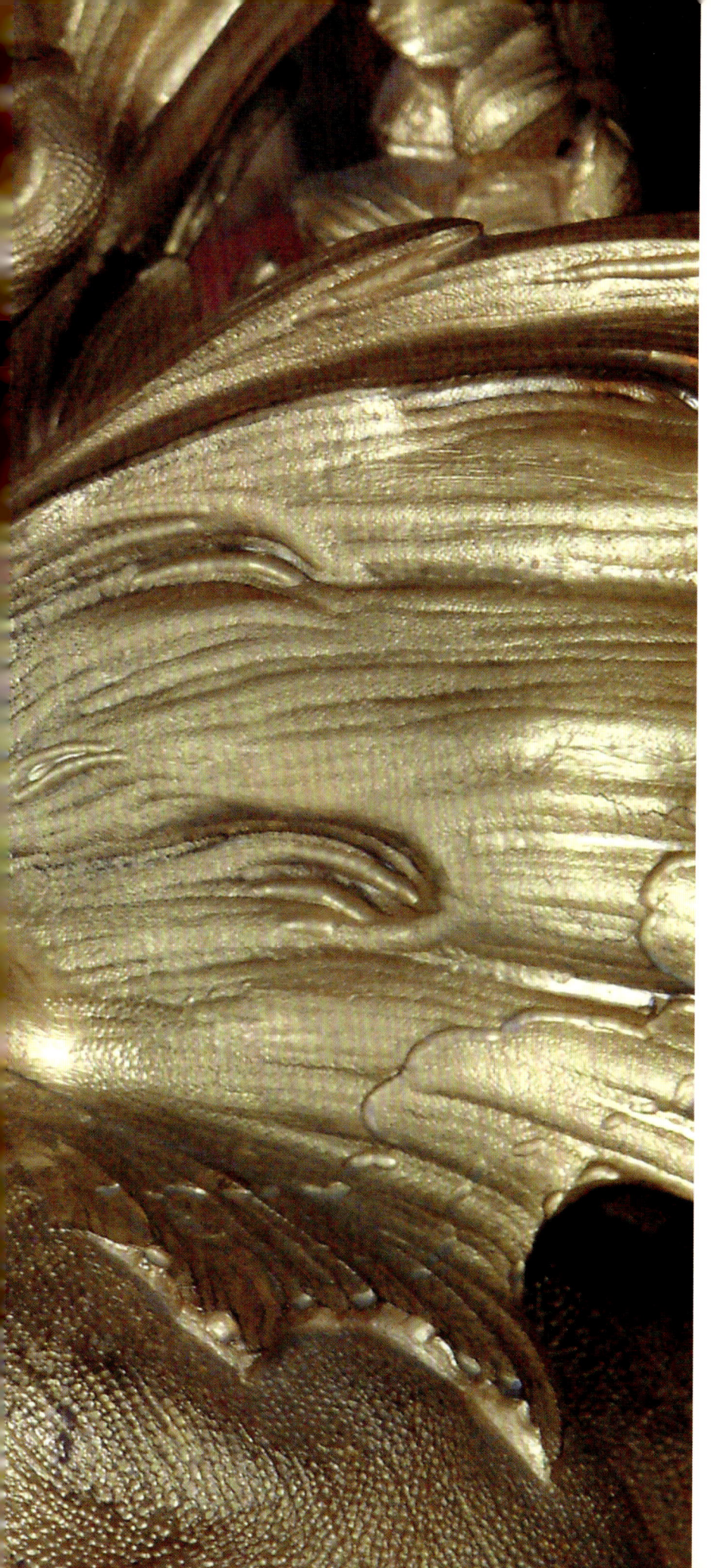

CHAPTER SIX

Trevor and Alexis Traina Residence
Pacific Heights, San Francisco

THE CREATION OF A GREAT FAMILY RESIDENCE can take many twists and turns. Thinking boldly and in Technicolor leads to adventures, discoveries, and the house of your dreams.

Trevor and Alexis Traina made highly ambitious plans to turn their newly acquired, rather sedate 1905 brick mansion overlooking San Francisco Bay into a worldly and welcoming home.

It is now the art-filled headquarters of a family on the go, as well as a backdrop for birthday parties, chic museum trustee gatherings, quiet lunches for the nuns whom Trevor advises on business matters, fundraisers, and children's games.

The dark brown brick house, which stands high on a granite hilltop (an essential foundation during the Great Earthquake of 1906 as well as subsequent earthquakes and tremors), had belonged to one family for almost a century. Its classic style was elegant and well mannered, and the couple intended to maintain that integrity. But its patinated rooms lacked certain amenities that are essential for art collectors, busy bloggers, a growing family, and a vibrant social life. Alexis, the creative director for Swanson Vineyards, her family's notable winery in the heart of Napa Valley, writes a witty blog that details her favorite tips and treats in the region. Trevor is a tech entrepreneur.

Trevor and Alexis loved many things about the house: its nod to classic Georgian taste, the grand mullioned bay window on the east side, its graceful proportions. It was close to perfect.

Their first act was to partially demolish the front wall, making way for creaking, rusty old excavation machinery to chomp at the front garden, throwing dust and rocks, and sending shattering vibrations and decibels of destruction in all directions. Within days, the demolition derby and deft use of dynamite was completed, and Trevor had gained three thousand square feet of subterranean space to show his art collection.

Inside the granite rock foundation there was also room for a larger garage, an elevator, a new entry, and a whimsical new glass conservatory made in England.

As the rock drilling ended and the two-year building renovation began, the Trainas started working with both the great New York–based decorator Thomas Britt, a longtime family friend, and Ann Getty, a friend and, as it happens, neighbor.

"We wanted to work with Ann because she has such a knowledge of design and especially of classical interiors that can be kicked up with modern art," said Alexis. "She has a fine-tuned talent for perfect scale, and like Trevor and me, she loves the exploration of color, fantasy, beauty, new ideas, wit, and humor."

The Trainas have both been exposed to outstanding interiors but wanted to learn more. "Ann has studied design and antiques for much of her life, she continues to be a scholar of antiques and art, and she has seen all the best of the great interiors," said Trevor. "She focused on how we would be using our rooms—and she orchestrated everything to make it all work."

Like other clients and friends, Alexis quickly discovered that working with Getty means taking advanced studies in textiles, every period of furniture, porcelain, china, silver, architecture, art, and objects.

For the Trainas she opened her decades-old list of purveyors she knows intimately and has employed: carvers in Mill Valley, gold-leaf specialists in San Francisco, lacquer experts in the San Fernando Valley and San Francisco's Chinatown, and a textiles atelier in Venice.

"Anything could be sketched, explored, attempted," Trevor recalled of Getty's vast list of specialists. The twenty-first-century version of a conservatory steeped in tradition? Ann understood the concept, and now it looks as if it had been there since 1905.

Trevor, knowledgeable about design and at the same time preoccupied with how and where to hang his growing photography collection, was totally involved in the process. "I will never forget Ann surrounded by two dozen piles of textiles, many layers deep, all arranged by color in the middle of the vast hardwood floor of what would someday become our children's playroom," recalled Trevor. "She had pulled them out of her design firm's orderly plastic bins and was leading my wife and me through the little mountains of color while studying our responses. Would there be a blue bedroom? Here were three velvets and a bright cotton that worked. How about a green study? Like them or not. She was pushing nothing. Just listening."

Alexis recalled that under Getty's guidance and tutelage, the couple placed graphic modern photography in their romantic bedroom and learned to be quite understated with color. They allowed some rooms, like the conservatory and the upstairs foyer, to remain quite monochromatic. Other rooms lift the spirits with acid green, Venetian red, shocking pink, magenta. The house is successful because it does not look like instant decor, and while it was brought together in a brief time span, it has the air of a house that grew and evolved.

"Ann encouraged us to dare to dream boldly," said Alexis.

On a foggy afternoon, the sound of children's laughter floats down from the nursery on the top floor. Cooking aromas waft lightly from the kitchen. Alexis is completing the week's blog post. Their Jack Russell, Tippy, snuffles on the stairway. Trevor arrives home early from his Jackson Square office. Today the rooms of the Traina residence glow with happiness.

TREVOR AND ALEXIS DUG DEEP INTO THE GRANITE HILLSIDE to create space for the new conservatory, *previous pages*, which is perched above the garage. The decor for this versatile Amdega garden room (often called an orangerie) is pure white with a jolt of lime green.

Ann Getty gives her clients full credit for the green accent in the conservatory. They wanted the room to be young, fun, and fresh. "The best design is always a collaborative effort, fully incorporating the client's lifestyle and personality," said Getty.

The green chenille fabric on the white chairs, pillows, and side chair is "Lana" in lime from Michael Taylor Designs. The Branch settee and bench, right, are from the Ann Getty House collection and were hand carved in alderwood, with an antiqued white finish. The original designs were created in 1938 by Elsie de Wolfe, who had them made by the House of Jansen for her Circus Ball, held at the Villa Trianon at Versailles. The quirky design of the custom-crafted Mulliner octagonal table with fitted chairs—from the Ann Getty House collection—was based on an English card table, circa 1745. The original was in walnut and featured fine decorative treatment in the carving detail. The doors open onto a terrace.

THE STATELY EAST-FACING FOYER—a kind of intermezzo between the intellectual stimulation of the photography galleries downstairs and the light-hearted family rooms upstairs—is one of the few sections of the house that was not remodeled or redecorated, *opposite*. With its marble floors and one small marble table, it's a study in restraint and classicism. No decoration needed.

BANQUETTES AND FOLDING CHAIRS IN THE DINING ROOM
were Ann Getty's idea. She had perfected the combination in her former New
York apartment, which had a somewhat small dining room. This plan chez
Traina keeps the middle of the room clear and offers the choice of pushing
the tables together, using just one small table, or clearing the chairs and tables
for a cocktail party. The chairs, quite sturdy, are upholstered in a Bergamo
fabric. Banquettes are upholstered in a custom-colored version of Sabina Fay
Braxton's printed velvet, Sang Sacre Delacroix. The folding chairs (inspired by
chairs from an Italian palazzo music room) are in the Ann Getty House collection. The peacocks, a gift from Trevor's stepmother, Danielle Steel, were from
Deyrolle, the Paris temple of taxidermy. Andrew Fisher designed the abalone-
topped pair of tables. The ferns are from Birch by Torryne Choate, Alexis's
favorite floral designer, who also designed the flowers elsewhere in the house.

THE DE YOUNG MUSEUM IN SAN FRANCISCO (one of the Fine Arts Museums of San Francisco) recently selected more than one hundred works from Trevor Traina's notable photography collection for an exhibition. In the exhibition's thought-provoking essays, the curators cited his selections as a prism for illustrating new trends in photographic realism.

Trevor's collection contains a number of the iconic works of the twentieth century, including Diane Arbus's *Identical Twins, Roselle, New Jersey, 1967* and William Eggleston's *Red Ceiling*. His selections highlight ideas, directions, and attitudes of the present day with works by photographers Andreas Gursky, Richard Prince, Jeff Wall, Cindy Sherman, Robert Rauschenberg, and John Baldessari. Images by such San Francisco natives as Larry Sultan, Peter Stackpole, and Ansel Adams are among the fast-growing collection, presented in several light-controlled galleries and rooms of the house.

THE BEDROOM, WHICH STRETCHES ACROSS THE NORTH-FACING TOP FLOOR of the house, includes a sunny conversation grouping around the limestone fireplace, and a chat sofa at left, punctuated with a pair of raw-wood Venus chairs from the Ann Getty House collection. The original circa-1800 chair in Ann and Gordon Getty's private collection is a very grand and formal Austro-Hungarian ormolu-mounted mahogany and parcel-gilt armchair. Adorning this chair are attributes of Venus, goddess of love, including the scallop shell, flaming torches, and the roses that decorate the back legs. Ann Getty redesigned this chair from the original, and the Trainas decided they loved the raw-wood, unpainted, and ungilded chair just as it arrived from the carver's studio. It's less formal and more modern.

The faux bois–paneled walls are by San Francisco–based Karin Wikström, known for her refined finishes and artistry. The bed features custom-made cast-bronze "twig" framing by San Francisco artist Andrew Fisher. Manuel Canovas Siam printed cotton was used for the canopy and curtains. Portraits are by Jackie Nickerson, a former fashion photographer based in New York and Ireland. This series of images features farmers in Zimbabwe, and textiles are evident. The Trainas love the style and humanity of Nickerson's work.

LAYERS OF ANTIQUES COMBINED WITH MODERN ARTISTRY give the Trainas' bedroom its sense of visual delight. The richly japanned and gilded eighteenth-century Venetian secretaire, a family heirloom, offers a sense of detail and architecture to the room. The painted chair is also Venetian.

THE OVAL BATHROOM, WHICH IS WASHED IN SUNSHINE for most of the day, was a key selling point for the house. Ann Getty likens the feeling in this room—Alexis's private bath—to "girly-vamp subtle" with a dash of va-va-voom in the classically theatrical English brass fittings. It is reminiscent of early 1940s movies but feels fresh and youthful. The curtain fabric is Osborne and Little's Perroquet, a cotton print designed by Nina Campbell. The designer's artful pattern of colorful parrots, pink roses in full bloom, and ornamental cherries was inspired by the Parisian floral boutique Odorantes on rue Madame on the Left Bank, which often features elegant taxidermy birds. The faux-bois walls and window frames (like the bedroom paneling) were painted by Karin Wikström.

ALEXIS AND TREVOR TRAINA WANTED THE BEDROOM SUITE to be a comfortable retreat where they could sit and read with their children or sip tea or Swanson wine with close friends. With this in mind, Getty created an inviting seating arrangement beside the fireplace. The plush textured magenta chenille armchairs—with Glant fabric from the Quinnault collection—swivel to offer extra versatility. The delicate faux bois–painted wall panels are by Karin Wikström.

IN TREVOR TRAINA'S OFFICE, WALLS ARE UPHOLSTERED IN ETRO VELVET CORDUROY, *overleaf.* In an inspired and cohesive scheme, the 1950s chairs from designer Val Arnold were also upholstered in the same Etro fabric. The graphic carpet is by David Hicks. California designer Val Arnold was also the source for the tiger maple desk, a Traina family heirloom, which offers its own graphic punch.

Trevor has been collecting Western and California paintings and furniture since he was a teenager, and one of his earlier bachelor residences in San Francisco was decorated with fine examples that now hang on these office walls. In his collection are paintings by Olaf Wieghorst, Joseph Henry Sharp, and Maynard Dixon. The vivid Sharp painting *Indian in Firelight* was purchased from Christie's as a graduation present from Trevor's mother.

THE FREDERIC REMINGTON BUCKING BRONCO ON THE DESK was a gift from his late father, John Traina, and his former stepmother, Danielle Steel. The painting behind the desk is *Sonoma Night* by Kim Wiggins, a New Mexico artist. The 1950s lamps were discovered in a Napa Valley antique gallery, since closed. The library table is vintage Stickley.

CHAPTER SEVEN

A House Near Lafayette Park
Pacific Heights, San Francisco

THE DUTCH MOTHER-OF-PEARL FLORAL BOUQUET INLAY that decorates a circa-1865 English cabinet, *previous pages*, stands near the Tiffany window in the dining room of this San Francisco residence, decorated by Ann Getty. The mother-of-pearl-inlay panel has a fascinating history. Created by the Dutch artist Dirck van Rijswijck, the original circa-1660 panel depicted elaborate floral garlands, luscious fruit, insects, a parrot, and memento mori objects including a winged hourglass, a broken sword, fallen crowns, and a laurel wreath. The moralistic message, typical of Northern European art of the time, is that life is fleeting, and glory and beauty fade. The inlaid design is set in slate. The panel was incorporated into a circa-1865 ebony- and brass-inlaid Boulle cabinet for Baron Lionel de Rothschild, and was in the Rothschild family London residences until 1937, when it was sold. Ann Getty won it at a later auction in London.

THE LIVING ROOM IS A VIVID ILLUSTRATION OF ORIENTALIST SPLENDOR. With its richly colored plaster walls, a late-nineteenth-century Agra carpet, limpid mirrors, a faint scent of amber, and elaborately ruched, tufted, and pillowed chairs and sofas, the living room fully realizes the oriental mood. The circa-1880 Victorian armchair in the foreground was acquired at a Christie's South Kensington sale.

Other delights include a George III japanned and parcel-gilt cabinet, left, and an Imari baluster jar and domed cover, and on the cabinet, left, a seventeenth-century Persian tulip vase. To delight the eye: lacquer-covered bowls on ormolu tripod stands, and nineteenth-century blue and green gilded Venetian chairs upholstered with tapestry. A pair of Kashmiri brass and enamel vases and two blue and white Kangxi porcelain vases, Qing dynasty, have been fitted as lamps. A water-gilded table stand with a top inset with a gilt-edged Berlin Seger porcelain plate was custom-crafted by Rossi Antiques, San Francisco. Getty's treasured textiles are here, including antique Lyon silks. All is order and beauty, luxury, peace, and pleasure.

FOR ANN GETTY IT'S ALL IN THE DETAIL AND LAYERS OF DELIGHTS. A rare Kangxi twelve-panel Coromandel screen dated "seventh month of 1659" is ornamented with mythical animals, battle scenes, legendary forests, clouds, and royal figures. The late Victorian mahogany billiard room sofa is upholstered in traditional Indian and Turkish silk-embroidered fabrics and crimson silk velvet. On the eighteenth-century lacquer panel table depicting Chinese sages caught in a storm is an Imari platter with a European sailing ship as a central motif. At right, the rare Chinese export/Portuguese giltwood and lacquer table, circa 1760, has a frieze carved and pierced with delicate scrolling leaves.

INTERIOR DECORATION IN ISTANBUL AT THE turn of the nineteenth century was a lavish and color-drenched homage to the French Orientalist style of the Second Empire. Later, Istanbul palaces and townhouses included a splash of *le style Rothschild* and a dash of Victorian dalliance.

Ann Getty visited these rich and delicious inspirations for the opulent and superbly detailed decor of a client's house in Pacific Heights. (The client has Turkish heritage.)

The simple, understated exterior of the residence, which was built in 1900, hardly suggests its hyper-romantic mood. In 1922 the house was used as a music studio, and a grand piano in the living room continues this tradition.

The exterior was modernized in the 1970s, but the interior's period details remained intact. Getty does not like to fight the architecture of a building and decided to incorporate Victorian elements into her design. *Le style Rothschild*, beloved in the salons of Paris and in glittering Istanbul palaces within sight of Topkapi Palace, pervades. French and English antique furniture, Persian and

fine Orientalist paintings in the style of Jean-Léon Gérôme, colorful carpets, cut-velvet textiles, and hand-woven silks were collected to enhance the rooms. Padded banquettes and armchairs add to the comfort.

The Second Empire's ambitious conquests stretched from Mexico to Egypt, just as the Ottoman Empire spanned continents. This aesthetic (like the Arts and Crafts movement) artfully blends Egyptian revival and the Orientalist with the Gothic, Louis XV, and Louis XVI revivals.

Getty deftly and elegantly combined the seraglio with salon opulence, embraced rare collections, and added the distinctive colors of exquisitely crafted Persian and Chinese pottery, as well as embroidered textiles from Rajasthan and Uzbekistan. Like Istanbul itself, which spans worlds and cultures, these rooms are opulent, comfortable, colorful, sophisticated, and elaborately patterned. As the western sun shimmers across the gilt chairs and blue and white pottery, guests almost expect to catch a glimpse of the Bosphorus from the front windows.

THE UPSTAIRS STUDY IS EQUALLY IN THE NINETEENTH-CENTURY TURKISH TASTE, paying homage to English and French refinement within sailing distance of the Blue Mosque. Gilded winged busts and gilded lions' paw feet give a sense of exoticism to a pair of early-nineteenth-century English Regency giltwood chairs in the manner of Henry Holland (opposite). As a counterpoint to the plush Ann Getty Home collection ottoman, foreground, and the delicate French circa-1800 bronze and gilt wall lights, are a pair of framed Rayonnist drawings, circa 1913, by the Russian artist Natalia Goncharova (1881–1962). The marble-topped Empire-style jardinière table, right, is French.

The stained-glass window was purchased in 1995 at a Sotheby's auction (above). It was attributed to the Tiffany Studio, but then the craftsmen installing the handsome stained glass wall panel in the dining room made a fortunate discovery. When the iron frame was disassembled, they found the authentic Tiffany Studio signature. The Favrile glass landscape window was crafted circa 1900, with poplars, mountains, and rhododendron flowers depicted in shades of striated and mottled opalescent glass. Also with a dramatic provenance is the mother-of-pearl-inlaid cabinet beside the window, which was made by Blake of London cabinetmakers, circa 1863, for Baron Lionel de Rothschild. The vanitas-inlaid slate panel set into the cabinet was by the Dutch artist Dirck van Rijswijck, circa 1660. The Victorian walnut and upholstered sofa stands on a carpet with a 1902 design by T.A.C. Colebrander. Getty acquired it at a Christie's Amsterdam sale. The eighteen English Regency–style dining chairs are simulated rosewood and parcel gilt with cane seats.

CHAPTER EIGHT

A House in Pacific Heights
San Francisco

AN ELABORATE 1755 GEORGE II GILTWOOD and plaster overmantel mirror with rocailles, chains of flowers, and small platforms for porcelains adds a frisson of glamour above the marble fireplace in the living room, *above.* On the mantel, a spinach-green late-eighteenth-century Chinese jade altar garniture includes candlesticks, a pair of beakers, and a censer on tripod legs. The setting is carved in the Moghul taste, with a flourish of lotus blossoms and leaves, and fitted with ornate gilt-metal stands.

To the left of the fireplace, *opposite,* the charming Impressionist painting is *Mother and Child* by Henri-Baptiste Lebasque (1865–1937). A pair of Qing dynasty Qianlong (1736–95) porcelain famille rose vases stands at left on the upper shelf of the secretaire, with two seventeenth-century Chinese porcelain carpet weights at right. Also on the shelves is a pair of Royal Worcester vases featuring flying phoenixes in the Oriental style, 1913.

The nineteenth-century European brass-mounted polychrome- and gilt-painted leather trunk depicts a court lady and her attendants, with a swirl of golden birds and dragons in the Chinese style. The wool knotted-pile Axminster carpet, of Savonnerie design, features floral bouquets and shell motifs.

A DARK BROWN AND POLYCHROME-DECORATED eighteenth-century Chinese Coromandel screen depicts floral motifs and trees along with courtly figures and mountain landscapes *(opposite)*. The reverse is decorated with exotic birds and cherry blossoms. The pair of ebonized and parcel-gilt corner tables is mid-nineteenth-century Chinese. The sofa and chair are Ann Getty Home designs.

WHEN A BELOVED MEMBER OF THE GETTY family and her daughters moved to a pretty Victorian-style house in Pacific Heights, Ann Getty decorated it with a ravishingly romantic master bedroom, collections of Chinese porcelains, Impressionist paintings, and a historic dining room of notable and rare provenance (see page 232).

It's a polished background for cocktail parties and quiet dinners, as well as homework, sleepovers, and birthday parties. Ann Getty's passion for Chinese and French antiques—and the many pleasures of chinoiserie—is played out on a smaller scale with finesse and understated ease. The dining room wall panels were discovered in Paris.

A DREAMY ESCAPE, THE BEDROOM WAS DESIGNED IN TONES OF IVORY, with delicate silks and antique gilded and painted furniture. The bed, sofa, and chairs were acquired at the Sotheby's 1999 auction of the furnishings of tastemaker Charles de Bestegui's legendary Chateau de Groussay and reupholstered. A pair of circa-1760 painted wood and ormolu encoignures (corner cabinets) is decorated in chinoiserie scenes on a pale background, and the legs display rocaille-cast mounts. The geometric design of the frieze suggests the beginning of neoclassicism of the period. On the bed canopy, an Italian giltwood triple-ray looking glass in the Directoire style, from a New Orleans auction, adds elegance and structure to the silken fabric. Two rock-crystal lamps are from the late twentieth century. Adding luster to the decor, Ann Getty selected a virtuoso pair of mid-eighteenth-century giltwood mirrors with ho-ho bird cresting and lilies. Four candle sconces enhance the fantasy and enchantment of this lovely room.

CHAPTER NINE

Todd and Katie Traina Residence
Presidio Heights, San Francisco

WHEN FILM PRODUCER TODD TRAINA, his wife, Katie, and their daughter, Daisy, moved back to San Francisco after a sojourn in Los Angeles, they commissioned Ann Getty to help decorate their new house. They wanted lighthearted decor, with a touch of Getty glamour.

As it happens, their classical house, perched on the crest of a hill, was built by renowned architect Willis Polk, who also built the Gettys' house.

The Trainas' house was built in the early 1920s. Over the decades it underwent many transformations, reflecting changing tastes and trends. During one springtime the house provided the location for the prestigious San Francisco Decorator Showcase. In the 1960s the owners built an indoor squash court, which the next owner turned into a screening room and the subsequent owner turned into an indoor lap pool. The Trainas filled the pool in and adapted the large room into a ballroom-size club, fashioned after New York's El Morocco supper club as a tribute to Todd's father, John Traina, a lifelong habitué of the chic spot. Banquettes and chairs were covered in dark blue and white zebra-patterned upholstery, with faux palm trees hovering above, just like the original, which opened in the 1930s.

The Trainas' art collection includes contemporary and pop art: Andy Warhol, Roy Lichtenstein, Claes Oldenberg, Wayne Thiebaud, Ira Yeager, and Sam Francis. Katie loves pottery, and Ann Getty, an expert on Chinese porcelains, gathered a dramatic collection of orange and blue Jindezhen pieces for her.

"We wanted the house to be relaxed, playful, with a bit of wit," said Todd. "We gather for drinks with friends on the banquette in the living room, and Daisy and her friends play there. We don't want to be too formal."

They selected a classic Scalamandré graphic zebra wallpaper for the guest powder room, in homage to Gino restaurant on Lexington Avenue and 61st Street in New York City, a beloved haunt of the couple that features the same design. Animals are a favorite motif, with a giraffe-patterned rug in the red library, a crystal antler chandelier in the dining room, a pair of dramatic Tony Duquette resin tusks at the front entry, and leopard-patterned fabrics in the living room.

In Getty's hands, the house is a blend of dramatic and playful, wrapped in a sophisticated package.

THE ENTRY HALL AND STAIRS ARE ORIGINAL TO THE WILLIS POLK–DESIGNED HOUSE, untouched through many decades of adapting and remodeling. Tony Duquette, a longtime family friend, provided the handsome pair of faux elephant tusks for the space, *previous pages*.

A PAINTING OF A TIGER BY NAPA VALLEY ARTIST IRA YEAGER, a family friend, swims above the coffee table, *opposite*. On the table is a collection of vintage flambé porcelain from Jindezhen, the legendary center of handcrafted Chinese porcelain for more than 1,800 years. Ann Getty acquired these rare pieces some years ago when she was on a porcelain sleuthing and buying trip in the region. *Above*: Ann Getty designed the tufted banquette to sweep around the bay window and provide comfortable seating for parties and celebrations. Vivid silk-velvet pillows and leopard-printed slipper chairs create a party-ready atmosphere.

CHAPTER TEN

Entertaining

CHRISTMAS SEASON AT THE GETTY RESIDENCE

is an especially festive and jubilant time—as December marks Gordon's birthday and that of his eldest granddaughter, Ivy.

Ann Getty brings together her creative teams in the fall to dream up concepts and sparkling décor (with past themes including Hollywood glamour, India, and China). The family's chef brings forth her *batterie de cuisine* to start weeks of work on feasting for all tastes.

On the appointed evenings, family members and friends of long and dear acquaintance mingle with the Gettys' favored mix of leaders in the arts, opera singers, fashionable grandes dames, tech and financial geniuses, fashion designers, winemakers, social activists, anthropologists, elected officials of many stripes, off-duty police officers, authors, dancers, musicians, Nobel Prize winners, and accomplished people in many fields.

One guest recalls magicians strolling among gilded armchairs of noble provenance in the living room, performing sleight-of-hand amusements. Alice in Wonderland and the Mad Hatter bantered nearby, so perhaps it was a trick of her imagination. It's all great fun.

Guests arrive at the Getty residence in highly original costumes—often custom-made for the occasion. Gordon cuts his birthday cake and sings wholeheartedly with guests.

Family members still recall the sumptuous fragrance one year when archways in the entry hall and living room were lavishly adorned with Della Robbia garlands and bowers of gardenias, fresh bay leaves, and lemons. Another year, the same party designer, Stanlee Gatti, a Getty favorite, created romantic Baroque columns and trellises intertwined with jasmine vines and opulent pale pink and white garden roses.

The indoor pool overlooking the garden is covered so guests can dance there to a rock group, a 1950s girl band, or a quintet playing soulful Paris cabaret favorites. The world of music is tapped, with tango, reggae, salsa, 1950s classics, and current hits.

For a recent December fete, the family invited artisan cheesemakers from Northern California to set up an elegant tasting table in the enclosed garden, offering perfectly ripe cheeses with accompanying handcrafted breads, dried California fruits and nuts, and condiments. Some guests say they still dream of that delectable cheese selection and the monogrammed natural linen napkins.

ORNAMENTS COLLECTED OVER MORE THAN THIRTY YEARS include commissioned figures from the Gettys' favorite operas: miniature Turandot, Romeo, and Juliet figures, along with Falstaff, Tosca, Otello, and Carmen. Joining in, with an operatic *sprezzatura*, are lifelike Gordon and Ann Getty figures holding rolls of parchment music scores. *Opposite:* Ann Getty has alighted on the thirteen-foot Christmas tree, thanks to the late interior designer Eleanor Ford, who commissioned the opera-inspired mouse-sized figures. The delicate characters in this series, about 175 in all, were sculpted by Homer Stenios in Hawaii and painted exquisitely by still-life artist Al Proom (display director at Gump's in San Francisco in the 1950s), then dressed by Frank Morales using textiles from costumes retired from the venerable San Francisco Opera.

ONE OF THE MOST ENTRANCING HOLIDAY TABLE SETTINGS WAS INSPIRED BY ANN GETTY'S LIFELONG LOVE OF CHINOISERIE.
This classical favorite pays homage to the romantic ideal of Chinese decor and design in the manner of the grand eighteenth-century English country houses. Party decor for this holiday dinner was a fantasy of far-distant Chinese courtly life, vividly depicted in seventeenth-century wall panels (from a Dresden palace of King Augustus the Strong, Elector of Saxony) in the dining room. Standing tall among the wine glasses are porcelain figures and objects, some precious and some recently reproduced in China. Getty is known for her often-arcane sources of world-class artists and craftspeople that work in the traditional manner. Her design office keeps files of private specialty workshops that will custom-craft porcelains, weave velvet and silk on hand looms, or create marquetry or craquelure finishes to her very exacting requirements and standards. *Opposite:* The paneled chinoiserie wall, visible above, has been electronically moved and concealed in the wall, left. Following dinner, guests walk into the music room for after-dinner drinks and a recital.

GETTY GATHERED EVERY ALLURING CHINA-RELATED OBJECT AND TEXTILE in her collections, including shimmering candlesticks, plates with Chinese motifs (hand-painted in Germany), and China trade decorations. The ensemble here—the hallucinogenic light-laden tree, the poetic table, vivid purple orchids and wrapped gifts, the jolts of color—made for a high-spirited celebration. Of special note are fashion-forward colors generated and inspired by the porcelain figures: vivid turquoise, magenta, tea rose, peach pink, apple green, and royal blue. For the family, the table setting was a wink and a nod to San Francisco's beloved Chinatown and its traditions of exuberant colors, crafts, and exoticism.

Guests at Getty parties linger on into the night, dancing, singing, and engaging in intense conversations. It has been whispered that on several occasions, young guests have been found sleeping on grand silk brocade tufted sofas in the living room early the next morning. They are very gently awakened—only to return the following year, of course.

Ann Getty says that a favorite way to entertain on weekends (especially Sunday evenings, which is a tradition chez Getty) is informally cooking with friends and sitting around the large table in the kitchen and eating family style. "I enjoy getting involved with the preparation, especially the baking. We hardly ever have leftovers because everyone wants to take the cookies home," she said.

THE DAZZLING CHINOISERIE DINING ROOM
was installed in a Getty family member's residence in San Francisco. The room is a multidimensional fever dream of mesmerizing eighteenth-century red and black painted panels punctuated with porcelain Buddha figures holding aloft gilt-bronze candelabra. It's furnished with mid-eighteenth-century Italian side chairs from Ven House, UK. The wall panels, complete with 1690 Chinese porcelain urns and lids for three-dimensional decoration, were discovered by Ann Getty and her longtime design associate, Maria Quiros, at the elegant Fremontier antique gallery on Quai Voltaire in Paris. They were then brought to San Francisco and adapted to fit into the space.

THE DECOR IS COMPRISED OF CHINESE LACQUER PANELS MADE IN CANTON with gold decorations and fruit and floral festoons on a black and red background. To obscure a window in the room, artist Agnes Yau painted an additional chinoiserie panel using the *verre églomisé* technique. The concept of this recherché style of room, interpreting Chinese arts in the European style and detailed with panels, brackets, niches, and porcelains, was directly influenced by French architect Daniel Marot, a contemporary of Louis XIV. Marot was appointed to the Dutch royal court and was credited with inventing this collector's cabinet style that became the rage for royal palaces in Europe.

THESE PORCELAIN VASES, LIDS, AND BOWLS IN THE EUROPEAN TASTE were manufactured in 1690 in Jingdezhen, China, and were then to be transported by the Dutch East India Company for clients in Holland via Canton and Jakarta. Off the shore of Vung Tau, a small island in Vietnam, the boat caught fire and sank with the precious cargo. It was not until 1989, when a fisherman discovered some of the pieces in his net, that arrangements were made to raise the boat and recover the cargo, mostly Kangxi blue and white porcelain, now encrusted with shells and barnacles. The pieces here had been packed in barrels and were rescued intact. Combining the porcelain with the paneling married objects that were destined to be together from the start.

GUESTS GATHER FOR DRINKS IN THE LIVING ROOM and then enter the dining room, here set for a fall dinner honoring illustrious scientists. The Getty family's Animalier dinner service was made in 1810 for the King of Holland. Eight Louis XV gilt chairs by Foliot circle the Regency-style dining table.

ACKNOWLEDGMENTS

DIANE DORRANS SAEKS

Directing and writing ANN GETTY INTERIOR STYLE and shooting all-new images has been an extraordinary journey, one that I pursued in privacy for the last several years.

Charles Miers, publisher of Rizzoli, championed this book and allowed me the freedom and structure to craft a beautiful and rare book. This is my sixth book for Rizzoli, and I am honored.

Dung Ngo, the great Rizzoli editor, was enthusiastic from the start and sent me on this adventure with confidence.

Alexandra Tart has been an exceptional editor. I admire and appreciate her refined eye, her elegance, her focus, and her "hands-off" approach to my writing. Working with her has been an extraordinary privilege.

Also at Rizzoli, the brilliant Pam Sommers, the executive director of publicity, and the wonderful Jessica Napp, associate director of publicity, are the best of the best, the top of the top. It is such a pleasure to work with Pam and Jessica.

To the fabulously talented art director Paul McKevitt at Subtitle New York, I send my warmest thanks and devotion. ANN GETTY INTERIOR STYLE is the sixth book Paul and I have worked on, and his great ability to create classic and understated design is one I admire enormously.

To Ann Getty, I owe my warmest thanks for the beauty of the worlds she has created, for her rare knowledge, for her sense of humor, and for her ongoing devotion to design and collecting. I have long been aware of the Getty family's cultural philanthropy around the world. Working on this book, I researched in depth Ann and Gordon's collections of the rare, the historically significant. I learned the importance of an emotional connection with each painting, sculpture, chair, chandelier, and object.

It has been my great pleasure to work closely with Taylor Nagle, Maria Quiros, Deborah Hatch, Monica Chavez, Claudia Rice, and Ann Getty's expert specialists, and I have valued their insights, remarkable knowledge, and devotion to this project. I am so grateful.

I worked closely with the great photographer, Lisa Romerein, on all-new photography, and I appreciate her technical skill and attention to detail. The beauty and emotion of her work graces the pages of this book.

Thank you to all the photographers whose glorious images enhance our knowledge of the Getty style.

As always, hurtling onward into the constant now. With thanks.

ANN GETTY AND ASSOCIATES ACKNOWLEDGMENTS

GORDON GETTY
DIANE DORRANS SAEKS

ANN GETTY AND ASSOCIATES STAFF:

Maria Quiros, Taylor Nagle, Beth Townsend, Monica Chavez, Patty Orr, Natalya Odvak, Marcella Canori, Christina Baruh, Agnes Yau, Sarah Moore, Fei Draper, Rob Corder, Ana Pekarovic

GETTY FINE ART STAFF:

Deborah Hatch, Claudia Rice, Brian Wheeler, Joni Stier

PHOTOGRAPHY:

Lisa Romerein, Yolanda White, Krista Ankeny, Francois Halard, Matthew Hranek, Ben Rose, Patrik Argast, Rachel Weill, David Duncan Livingston, Terry Lorant, Keith Morrison, Larry Sultan

DESIGNERS/ARCHITECTS:

Sister Parish, Albert Hadley, John Stefanidis, Leavitt Weaver, Ed McEachron, Erica Severns, Barbara Newsom, Jeanne Murphy, Eleanor Ford, Stanlee Gatti, Ron Herman

SOURCES:

Sabina Fay Braxton, Bevilacqua, Prelle, Antico Setificio, Robert Kime, Sotheby's, Christie's, Hildebrand Furniture, Campero Fine Furniture, Living Concepts, Rossi Antiques, Shears and Window, J Nelson Inc, Michael Taylor Designs, Christopher Hyland, Cadre, Mariner Pacific, Declercq Passementiers, Besselink, Jones and Milne Ltd, C. John, Keshishian, Stark Carpets, S. Francis, Kapoor Carpets, Lotus Collection, Francesca Galloway Ltd, Cora Ginsburg Inc, Spink & Sons, Mallet, Paul Reeves, Geoffrey Diner Gallery, Birch, Bloomers

ARTISTS, TRADES, CONTRACTORS:

Linda Horning, Shirley Robinson, Karin Wikstrom, Amy Van Avery, Frances Binnington, Carole Lansdown, George Noland, Scott Smith, Brent West, Al Proom, Ian Agrell, Adam Thorpe, Ev Thomas, Mayta Jensen, Frank Webb Construction, Muratore Inc, JMK Construction, Ryan and Associates, Allen Davis, Orion Construction Managers, Paige Glass, John Neumann, Steel Décor, Cirecast, Dusty Dillon, Andreas Marble, Clervi Marble, Russell and Boals Painting, Nolan Brothers Painting, Phoenix Woodworking, Luis Norori, Century Electric, Construction Audio Services, , Fatima Santana, Georgina Rice, Siteworks, Gander and White, Masterpiece International, Thomas Sullivan Transportation, Elwell Trucking, Lawrence Fine Art

RESTORATION:

Stair Restoration, Mark Harpainter, Tracy Power, Tony Rockwell, Antoinette Dwan, Janice Schopfer, James Durfee, Papillon Rug Care, Tatjana Kopp, Talisman Restoration

SPECIAL THANKS:

Greg McIntyre, John Nelson, Andrew Fisher, Jeffry Weisman, John Brewer, Gray Watkins, Sotheby's Experts, Roberta Louckx, Gillian Wilson, Brian Considine, Melissa Leventon, Yvette Robbins, Shelley Lim, Anacleto Gonzalez, Jose Gonzalez, Linda Gonzalez, Celestina Perez, Victor Campero, Torryne Choate, Pam Wolff, Virginia Sykes-Wright, Devereaux Smith, Kathryn Kimball, Dom Moreci, Cory Levenberg, Helga Horner, Michael Barcun, Warren Weitman, Giles Waterfield, Ulrich Leben, Martin Chapman